1

SEMINAR STUDIES IN HISTORY

Editor: Patrick Richardson

THE PROBLEM OF POVERTY
1660–1834

SEMINAR STUDIES IN HISTORY

Editor: Patrick Richardson

A full list of titles in this
series will be found on the
back cover of this book

SEMINAR STUDIES IN HISTORY

THE PROBLEM OF POVERTY
1660–1834

Geoffrey Taylor

Senior History Master
King's College School
Wimbledon

LONGMANS

LONGMANS, GREEN AND CO LTD
London and Harlow

ASSOCIATED COMPANIES, BRANCHES AND
REPRESENTATIVES THROUGHOUT THE WORLD

© Longmans, Green and Co Ltd 1969
First published 1969

SBN 582 31392 9

PRINTED IN GREAT BRITAIN BY WESTERN PRINTING SERVICES LTD, BRISTOL

Contents

Part Three · Assessment

Part Four · Documents

Introduction to the Series

The seminar method of teaching is being used increasingly in VI forms and at universities. It is a way of learning in smaller groups through discussion, designed both to get away from and to supplement the basic lecture techniques. To be successful, the members of a seminar must be informed, or else—in the unkind phrase of a cynic, it can be a 'pooling of ignorance'. The chapter in the textbook of English or European history by its nature cannot provide material in this depth, but at the same time the full academic work may be too long and perhaps too advanced for students at this level.

For this reason we have invited practising teachers in universities, schools and colleges of further education to contribute short studies on specialised aspects of British and European history with these special needs and pupils of this age in mind. For this series the authors have been asked to provide, in addition to their basic analysis, a full selection of documentary material of all kinds and an up to-date and comprehensive bibliography. Both these sections are referred to in the text, but it is hoped that they will prove to be valuable teaching and learning aids in themselves.

Note on the System of References:

A bold number in round brackets (**5**) in the text refers the reader to the corresponding entry in the Bibliography section at the end of the book.

A bold number in square brackets, preceded by 'doc.' [**docs 6, 8**] refers the reader to the corresponding items in the section of Documents, which follows the main text.

PATRICK RICHARDSON
General Editor

Acknowledgements

We are indebted to the following for permission to reproduce copyright material:

Cambridge University Press for an extract from *Seventeenth Century Life in the Country Parish* by E. Trotter.

Part One

BACKGROUND

1 The Restoration Inheritance

The poor comprised the majority of the population in the late seventeenth century. Yet they played little part in the political conflicts, the crisis of constitutional confidence, which has made the epoch the object of exhaustive and continuing study, and so have received relatively scant attention from the historian. Christopher Hill, indeed, refers to the mass of the population as 'surviving in records when they are born, married, accused of crime, or buried, but otherwise leaving no trace' (21). New historical thinking is revealing more, however, of the submerged masses, of those who did not belong to the 'political nation'. It is doing so by deeper investigation of such records as exist, concentrating on localities after the shining example of Dr Hoskins (24), but more than that, by sympathy and concern with social issues. Present day historians no longer work in a mere scholastic void, and their interests range beyond the well-worn paths of kings and ministers, of soldiers and churchmen. The poor, even 'the middling sort', hold their own intrinsic fascination, and furthermore illuminate the structure of the society they inhabited, as Rudé's pioneering work has made clear (38, 72).

The nature of English eighteenth-century society was noted among contemporaries, in Europe as in England, for its stability and relative harmony of classes. To a significant degree, this reflected the fact that the poor were the responsibility of all sections of the community: they could not, under the operative Elizabethan Poor Law, be herded out of sight. The eighteenth century, on the other hand, existed cheek by jowl with the poor, the infirm, the aged, the mentally sick. The village idiot was an everyday sight, the object of humour to minds unsophisticated by medical understanding. The situation of the poor must be observed in an environment of brutality, of public whippings and the pillory, of pain and discomfort, and of the necessity of 'bottom'. In such a barbarous atmosphere the indulgence with which the poor were regarded is almost curious.

3

The victory of the propertied classes over central government at the Restoration of 1660 made the leading figures of localities intimately aware of the incidence of poverty, and, in rural parishes, of the individuals who received benefit. The continuous involvement of whole communities in 'the greatest social problem of the day' gave a unity to the period of the Old Poor Law which stands acceptable comparison with other periods, other places. It must nonetheless be acknowledged that such commendation can only apply to the social conditions in which the Elizabethan Poor Law best worked; that is, to the rural parish. The town, especially London with its newly emergent phenomenon of 'the mob', posed a different set of problems, for which the Old Poor Law offered no remedy.

What, then, was the inheritance of 1660? The Poor Law of Elizabeth (43 Eliz. c. 2) provided the basis of administration until its total abolition in the Amendment Act of 1834. Despite changes enforced by the rapidly evolving industrial and agrarian complex, the essential provision of outdoor relief remained intact throughout these years, extended *ad absurdum* by the Speenhamland System [**doc. 12**]. The 1601 act had a threefold intention: to provide work for the unemployed, to educate and bind out as apprentices pauper children, and to relieve 'the lame, the impotent, the old, the blind, and such other among them being poor and not able to work'. The scope of the act widened considerably during the period up to 1834, to embrace contracts with local doctors in cases of sickness, and in providing funeral expenses (including tolling the funeral bell, and bread and beer for the bearers), paying rents or finding houses for the poor, and so on. In numerous ways the legislation was augmented to represent a widespread, if rudimentary, social welfare service. There was, however, no coordinated policy, no governmental initiative, and this absence of central control mirrored the character of the Restoration, and its corollary, the Revolution Settlement of 1689.

Power in the state, which had earlier radiated from the Court, now passed to a Parliament whose members represented individual parochial interests. The Stuart policy of centralism had met with the persistent opposition of the gentry: they had opposed Privy Council demands for returns from the parishes in 1631, and its attempted regulation of the corn market in times of scarcity. The goal of the Parliamentarian side in the Civil War was in large measure decentralisation.

Henceforth the self-sufficiency of each district, 'parochial laissez-faire', was to determine treatment of the poor, as control of the affairs of state fell to the independent gentry whose interests have been so meticulously catalogued by Professor Namier (35). No government, no minister, could afford to ignore their wishes down to the end of our period: independency was more prevalent than party alignment.

Largely, the Restoration confirmed the work of the Long Parliament. The broken weapons of conciliar government, Star Chamber and the Church courts were not refurbished by the Cavaliers. Where the Poor Law was concerned, there was hardly a trace of regulative monarchy. The government, in the face of this massive social problem, was paralysed, if not by inertia, then by lack of the instruments of government.

The *raison d'être* of absolutism was order; the fear of chaos was never far from the seventeenth-century mind. Cromwell himself sought vigorously for a foundation of order, and the unpopular and efficient expedient of the Major-Generals marked the last time in English history, before the nineteenth century, that local government was run from Whitehall. From this point, responsibility for law and order rested with the locally based magistracy, which was not brought to book by any overweening conciliar jurisdiction. Common law, costly and unconcerned with executing policy, was triumphant, and justices of the peace relapsed in 1660 into two centuries of virtual irresponsibility. What made the system effective at all was the harmony between themselves and a Parliament drawn from the same classes, representative of the same propertied interests. That the poor became less of a physical threat to the nation than in the past reflects some credit on their effectiveness. But then, they were autonomous, and financially interested.

The parish was, indeed, prepared to spend large sums of money in the courts to secure its rights to be delivered of paupers under the Act of Settlement [**doc. 3**]. Such interparochial contests were of little worth. The total number of the poor was not diminished, litigation impaired the self-respect of the pauper, and the costs of law suits became themselves a burden on the rates which the authorities were seeking to curtail. Yet the Act of Settlement had its justifications, among them a concern for domestic peace: it was in part designed to harry wandering discharged Ironsides. Towns, and especially London, filled with beggars. The preamble to the 1662 Act speaks of wandering vagabondage somewhat hysterically, but the absorption of 50,000 ex-soldiers posed a real problem to an inelastic rural society. There was no standing army, and the tenuous nature of the means of coercion must be weighed when assessing the harshness or otherwise of eighteenth-century Poor Law administration. It has often been suggested that the Poor Laws were implemented mainly to allay unrest and disorder. Certainly it was a principal requirement of post-Restoration government to protect private property.

No sketch of the background to the position of the poor would be complete without some reference to the massive contribution made by private charity in the years prior to 1660. W. K. Jordan (**27**) has provided a wealth of evidence, most strikingly perhaps of the overwhelming contribution (over 71 per cent) of the merchant classes. What must be noted by way of introduction is that the Poor Law's intention was of a minimal concept. The burden of relief was expected, under 43 Eliz. c. 2, to be borne by private individuals [**doc. 17**]. Public benefaction was extensively, if erratically, applied, and the extension of humanitarian sentiments in the latter half of that century requires consideration if the treatment of poverty is not merely to be allowed the restricted context of Poor Law administration.

The Old Poor Law, with its successive amendments and experimentation, was hardly the same administrative structure which derived from Tudor conciliar practice. But the essential feature which came under the hammer of the Utilitarian bureaucrats in the 1830s was much what the Restoration implanted: reliance on mainly outdoor relief, locally collected and locally administered.

2 Quantitative Factors

The statistical basis of the extent of poverty is inexact. Economics was in its infancy in the late seventeenth century, and those who began turning out pamphlets, the 'political arithmeticians', perforce relied on estimates. The first effective census of the whole population was taken in 1801, and compulsory registration of births, marriages and deaths, lies beyond our period, in 1836. In part, the lack of such essential information is the result of gentry interest: the intention of all government enquiry was open to the gravest suspicion, and the cry of an Englishman's liberty served as a defence mechanism for the heirs of the Revolution Settlement, the propertied classes. For liberty, it is cautionary to read privilege. If the central government investigated a man's household, such information was likely to be used for taxation purposes: of such a nature were the hearth tax returns, and this helps to account for eighteenth-century opposition to proposals for a census.

Nevertheless, available assessments serve to indicate the broad outlines of the problem. The questions of population increase, agrarian and industrial development, and the emergence of an urban civilisation, are closely related to the changing circumstances of the poor. Such changes produced a new kind of poverty, and social relationships were fundamentally altered.

The population of England and Wales increased from around $5\frac{1}{2}$ million in 1660, by stages, to 9,157,176 in 1801 (the year of the first census), and to 13,897,187 in 1831. This is a striking rise and an unequivocal statistic. What is less clear is why and how this came about. Perhaps the most important factor was the falling death rate. In 1740, 75 per cent of all children born were dead by their sixth year; at the beginning of the nineteenth century the percentage was 41. Falling death rates are the subject of most modern research, since birth rates showed only a marginal rise. The frequently cited improvement in medical conditions, however, is now seriously challenged as belonging to a later period. The use of new materials, of brick and tiles, more effective scavenging, the Great Fire of London —all these contributed to the decline of endemic plague. But the crucial cause, 'an obscure ecological revolution among rodents', is asserted to have been that the large outdoor brown rat replaced the domestic small black rat, having arrived in England by sea in the 1720s. It drove out its smaller rival, thereby replacing a 'free-wandering flea' (carrier of the bacillus) by a 'nest-loving flea' (**11**). Plague, in the terrifying form of cholera, returned to this country in epidemic proportions at the close of our period, entering the north-east ports in October 1831. It was again a black rodent which brought contamination.

What proportion of these growing numbers joined the ranks of the poor? Until 1776 there exist only the estimates of successive pamphleteers, men like Sir William Petty, who, under the new influence of scientific enquiry, sought to base inductive reasoning on statistical data. His difficulty, universally shared, was the absence of such data (**104**). By far the most important social statistician was Gregory King (**101**). He based his conclusions on a sampling of tax records, especially of hearth tax returns, and the modern experts have considered its findings broadly satisfactory. Of a population of 5·5 million, 1·3 million are described as 'Cottagers and Paupers', 30,000 as 'Vagrants, or Gypsies, Thieves, Beggars, &c.', and a further quarter of a million as 'Labouring People and Outservants' [**doc. 18**]. Thus, looking at Gregory King's figures conservatively, a quarter of the population was in a state of actual poverty; that is, having to spend more than they earned. This was a chronic condition, but one which reached even worse proportions in periods of trade depression, as in 1668 and the 1690s, or harvest failure, and might draw into the pauper host the artisan, small shopkeeper, innkeeper, apprentice, common soldier and seaman, making in all 3·3 million out of 5·5 million.

Yet at best, Gregory King could but estimate; the first really firm statistical information stems from Thomas Gilbert's enthusiastic enquiries. The returns of 1776 show a population of 7½ million, which had increased to 8 million by 1783, and the 1801 census confirmed this explosive surge. There was bound to occur a comparable increase in the numbers of the poor, given a ceiling of productivity, and indeed this did happen. From Gregory King, it has been seen that the potential poor numbered 3·3 million, or 60 per cent. Before

1834, according to Mark Blaug (55) 'we know next to nothing about the actual number of people relieved'. There were two attempts at a census of the poor, noisily accompanied by frequent subjective assessments. That of 1802 showed one million on relief, including 300,000 children under fifteen: that is, 11 per cent of the population came under the shelter of 43 Eliz. c. 2. Where, however, Gregory King confused his picture by counting farmers many times over, the census counted more than once any pauper who applied, as he commonly did, for relief on two or three occasions during the year. The attempt of 1812–14 is equally unsatisfactory, and failed to count the children under fifteen who were on outdoor relief. Worst of all, the New Poor Law was enacted on the basis of statistical ignorance, an ignorance which we must largely share. There was no attempt to take a census of the poor, no account of rural unemployment, 'no hint of a quantitative view of the problem', no synthesis of the returns. The 'principles of 1834', which were drawn from more hostile assertion, leave a sense of irritation that the new science of political economy should have left the record so avoidably confused.

It must therefore be considered that data is too fragmentary to be conclusive. Nonetheless, output growth, which dated from the 1740s, enabled the nation to survive, in some measure, the huge population increases noted. There was an important surplus in the economy of resources and of capital for investment. Moreover, it is interesting to note the comparison made by Phyllis Deane (11) between the poor of eighteenth-century England, and those of today's under-developed countries, based on national income data. She finds the earning capacity of eighteenth-century England to be twice that of present day Nigeria, and three times that of India. 'Crude and impressionistic' though her figures may be, they do indicate that there are gradations of poverty: even the overflowing American economy has poverty as its second front.

The terrifying possibilities of uncontrolled breeding struck men of the eighteenth century, as those of today, with force. After 1660 opinion was influenced by Dutch example. Hands rather than acres were regarded as the key to wealth as the acquisition of commercial empires and the growth of output enabled employment of the labour force. This optimistic viewpoint persisted until Thomas Malthus douched the prospect of employment capacity. His pamphlet (103) provoked widespread gloom about the nature of human progress, yet was founded on the now demonstrably false maxim that any

Background

productivity rise would be followed, and outpaced, by population rise. He regarded the Old Poor Law as a stimulus to large families. Though population growth was similar at this time in Scotland and Ireland, where Speenhamland did not operate to supplement earnings, and though Malthus himself modified his views, his prophesies continued to haunt future generations: the assumed interrelation between outdoor relief and population surplus largely worked to destroy the Old Poor Law.

The unit of administration, while varying widely in acreage and number of inhabitants, was for the most part extremely small. The 12,000 parishes and townships of 1660 had risen to 15,535 in 1831, in England and Wales and, allowing for the slow formation of some 200 autonomous statutory incorporations or unions for dealing with the poor, tiny communities in geographical isolation were the norm. Two thirds of the authorities were administering the needs of around 200 families each; even in 1831, 12,034 parishes supervised populations of under 800. The number must clearly have been substantially fewer in 1660.

Yet it was in the large town that the imperfection of the administrative procedure exposed itself. The great evil of 'congregation' really belongs to a later period (34), but it was the town which attracted the unemployed, the beggar, the vagrant. In the new towns they could find the sanctuary of anonymity, and it was in a tenement environment, mushrooming in the years up to 1834, that local paternalism worked least effectively. The amenders of 1834 concentrated on difficulties of the south, Speenhamland country; but it was in the industrial areas that the misery of poverty was being nurtured.

How dynamic was the growth of towns? In 1670 there were only two cities in England with over 50,000—London had 750,000, Bristol, 60,000. The bulk of towns in the seventeenth century were small market towns or little ports. By the time of the 1801 Census, London had reached 864,000, and had topped the million by 1811, when in addition, Manchester and Salford numbered 98,573, Liverpool, 94,376, Birmingham, 85,700, and Leeds, 62,500. Bristol's growth rate was somewhat slower, its population totalling 76,500 in 1811. Such conurbations introduced entirely new factors, for which Elizabethan enactment could not be legislatively or administratively effective.

The traditional view of rural depopulation is strongly challenged

10

by recent writers, and Chambers and Mingay (7) have retinted the prejudiced pictures which have filtered down to us through the writings of Crabbe and Goldsmith or the didactic assertions of the Hammonds and the Webbs (**17, 18, 19, 49**). The new husbandry absorbed rather than obviated labour; criticism of the poor rate burden was muted in times of high prices; the decline of the rural handicraft (with handloom weaving the classic illustration) threw more people 'on the parish' than did enclosure; Speenhamland developed in the low-wage areas of the south as a response to surplus labour, rather than being a cause of it: these number among recent conclusions. There was rural decay, but it was regionally confined.

It must be accepted that population rise, free of epidemic massacre, was a provocation to increased production. The modern industrial economy is distinguished by the association of sustained output and demographic growth. The evidence of acute poverty in the last decades of the Old Poor Law is overpowering; but its nature was periodic and regional, and depended on external factors outside the control of the small unit of pauper administration.

3 Costs

The expense of administering the Poor Law rose markedly during the period up to 1766, and spectacularly thereafter [**doc. 19**]. In the mid-seventeenth century, the Webbs (**49**) calculated, the total sum expended was £250,000 per annum, or one shilling per head of population. (By 1832 this had risen to £7 million, or ten shillings per head.) The amount probably doubled by the end of the seventeenth century, though contemporary pamphleteers, resentful of rapid increase resulting from the general distress of the country, estimated still higher figures. Doctor Davenant put it at £665,362, a figure 'Collected with great Labour and Expence by Mr. Ar.Mo. a very Knowing Person' (**88**), and agreed by Gregory King (**101**). Richard Dunning produced the pessimistic figure of £819,000, basing his calculations on Devon parishes (**91**). Other writers—there were many—asserted that the figure approached 'a million of money'. But the most reliable statistics came from John Locke's committee at the Board of Trade, which demanded a set of returns from the Church, 4,415 parishes, one third of the whole, submitted them, and the resultant figure assessed for the whole kingdom, amounted to £400,000, or less than a two shilling *per capita* contribution. Probably by the end of the century the poor rate was producing up to £700,000, and some yardstick may be that the Crown was voted a total income by the Cavalier Parliament of £1,200,000 for all government business —and even that was never collected.

Thomas Gilbert's returns, firm at last, revealed in 1776 an expenditure of £1,529,780; ten years later this expenditure had soared to £2,004,238, an increase of 33 per cent, and the largest decade increase of the century. The French Wars, and the generally-agreed hardships of the 1790s, brought further augmentation in the amount of relief given. In the return of 1803 the sum was £4,267,965, or 9 per head of population, while the optimum expenditure for 1818 reached almost 5·8 million, 13s 3d. per head, and one-sixth of total public expenditure. Thereafter the graph levelled out, even starting

a downward curve in the boom years of 1823–1826, to a final figure
of around £7 million, 10s per head. N. J. Silberling (**74**) calculated
that this represented only 2 per cent of an estimated gross national
income of £400 million, but this requires the qualification that the
burden fell solely on the ratepayers who were additionally supporting
numerous philanthropic projects.

Associated with the overall total of expenditure was the relative
contribution of Speenhamland and non-Speenhamland counties.
In 1802, 12s per head was contributed in the former, 8s in the
latter; in 1831 the proportion was 13s 8d to 8s 7d Professor
Clapham (**9**) discovered in 1926 that a Select Committee on Labourers' Wages of 1824 had listed many counties in the south (including
Hampshire, Kent, Surrey, Hertfordshire and Middlesex, inclusive
of London) which denied practising the Allowance System, while at
the same time the policy was found to operate in Nottinghamshire
and Northumberland, and the East and North Ridings. Nevertheless, even accounting for this, and that population statistics varied
between counties, a clear trend is seen of higher relief in agricultural
than non-agricultural counties, making relief under Speenhamland
appear uneconomic and strongly influencing the condemnatory view
of 1834.

The inclusive rise of costs followed an erratic course in the period
1660–1834, fluctuating wildly in periods of harvest difficulty and
trade depression.

Of this growing provision, contributions were assessed by the
parish authorities. The amount payable by each parish was fixed
by the churchwardens and overseers, and such charges fell only on
real property or tithes. By this method of levy, the urban manufacturers escaped responsibility for workers in hard times. Furthermore, only the occupier was assessed by the Churchwardens, and
the owner was not rated for the rents he received, or for any lands he
might hold outside the parish. There were other forms of rating,
which were disputed—especially whether a tradesman should be
taxed according to his stock in trade—and such questions went to
the courts for (often contradictory) decisions. If the amount of
money raised were insufficient to meet needs, the magistrates were
empowered under 43 Eliz. c. 2 to rate other parishes within the
Hundred. Parochial jealousy rarely permitted this course of action,
though it was a recourse applied in straggling northern parishes of
Lancashire, Yorkshire and Westmorland, and where each hamlet

13

appointed its own overseers. Unfair assessment, frequent in a system
which encouraged favouritism, was redressed by appeal to the
Quarter Sessions. It was yet another cumbersome feature of a system
which foundered on administrative chaos.

4 Parish Organisation

The mechanism of the parish afforded small prospect that pauper legislation would be effectively administered. The vestry or parish meeting stood as the unit of administration, transformed from a medieval ecclesiastical usage to an amateur agent of civil administration, the most important local government authority outside the City of London and the boroughs. Unpaid public service was the ideal which underpinned the system: in practice it was the legal compulsion to serve which enabled it to work.

Parish officers were untrained in public administration and appointed for one year only. They comprised the churchwardens, the overseers of the poor, the petty constable and the headboroughs. The only paid permanent officials were the vestry clerk, the beadle and the workhouse master or mistress.

The churchwardens, usually of gentry stock, were chosen annually by inhabitants of the vestry and were *ex officio* overseers of the poor. They shared with the overseers the responsibility for the payment of relief to paupers, though more often they provided for the needs of the casual poor. Long term relief was provided by the overseers of the poor, two to each parish, who were nominated by the vestry to the justices of the peace [**doc. 5**]. The petty constable was the linchpin of social life in rural England. Originally a servant of the manor, his role as a functionary had extended with the passing of time. He was not paid a salary, but in so corruptible an office there were naturally opportunities for taking fees, bribes and gifts. He was to protect private property, watch for vagabonds, prevent trespassing and poaching, keep the taverns and inns quiescent, catch petty thieves, arrange for illegitimate children, keep an eye on apprentices, and ensure the payment of local and national taxes. The constable was assisted in these manifold tasks by headboroughs, usually two in number.

The conduct of these untrained officials was subject only to the surveillance of the justices of the peace, who alone could examine any persons suspected of misdemeanours. They dealt with the parish on a local and personal basis at Petty Sessions, and on a county basis at Quarter Sessions. Justices examined paupers, potential or actual, and would authorise removal where a legal settlement was not proved. They further signed settlement certificates and apprenticeship indentures, appointed overseers and approved their accounts after they had passed in vestry, and allowed the assessments for their rates. This was usually a formality, though suspicion did at times show through, as at Westbury in 1700, 'allowed of this Account if true'. Appeals against removal, not commonly encountered for obvious reasons, were made to the magistrates in Quarter Sessions. Any real check on the malversation of funds was beyond the capacity of the magistracy.

Parishes frequently comprised more than one village, particularly in areas of low population density, and their extent ranged from thirty acres to thirty square miles. It was in the large, urban parish that corruption was most prevalent, for it was there that sustenance of shifting populations required large doles of money. The practice of contracting was especially open to speculation where 'select vestries' (that is, controlling finances, with only nominal supervision by the overseers) disposed of contracts among members of the vestry and their friends [**doc. 4**]. This was merely one burden stemming from maladministration: many sums paid out to itinerant paupers are dubiously vague, for example, 'To a poor person . . . 0.6*d*.; To a lame woman going to Worcester . . . 2.0*d*.; To one very ill . . . 5.0*d*.' On a grander scale, for the year 1714, in the parish of St Martin-in-the-Fields, such costs totalled £1,876 16*s* 4*d*. (**13**). Additionally, officers of the parish were accustomed to wine and dine out of the poor rate, at a changeover of officers, at ordinary vestry meetings, and on attending the bench. One beanfeast, again in the offending parish of St Martin's, cost in all £49 13*s* 9*d*. Such application of an expense account mentality appals, but it is fair to remember that officials were unpaid, and that they had a commitment to social service more extensive than anything encountered by the responsible citizen of the present: perhaps a little jollity was excusable after the supervision of the 'particular unloveliness of a pauper funeral'. What was inexcusable, however, was the system which allowed of such abuses [**doc. 6**].

Outdoor relief was the foundation of the Old Poor Law. This was dribbled out in weekly doles, at the discretion of the overseers, to the lame, impotent, old, blind, 'and such other among them being poor and not able to work'. Pauper children were lodged either with a woman or at a workhouse: 2s 6d per week was allowed for their upkeep, which was not ungenerous, given proper supervision by overseers. The range of relief was widened during the course of the eighteenth century by individual parochial initiative, to include payment of rent and provision of houseroom or houses; payment of funeral expenses for the pauper; supply of necessities for the needy, of food, fuel and clothes—a sympathetic overseer at Leytonstone in 1740 provided Beck Mitton with money 'to fetch hir stays out of pawn'.

Care of the sick was also adopted during the eighteenth century. Doctors were employed by the parish, increasingly on a contractual basis. It was clearly in the doctor's interest to keep his costs down once he had obtained his tender, but parishes were concerned to obtain value too, and the following, taken from the annals of Burton-on-Trent, is a salutary lesson in medical cost-effectiveness: '£10 agreed for the cure of Jacob Mossley the Younger, in case he shall make him sound and well. . . . No cure no pay. The money to be paid at the end of three months after he shall be reported cured.' The relative freedom from endemic plague has been noted previously, but authorities were still faced with serious health hazards, of which smallpox was the most common and dangerous before the cholera invasion, though somewhat giving way to vaccination after 1803, thanks to Jenner's free treatment of the poor. Added to this were the falling sickness, 'ye Itch', 'fitts', and lunacy. Bedlam, or the local House of Correction, was the general repository for lunatics, whose expenses for barbarous treatment had to be found out of the poor rates.

One administrative device sacrificed by post-Restoration parishes was the provision of stock for setting the 'able poor' to work, a primary aim of 43 Eliz. c. 2. But apart from providing poor parishioners with essential tools (mending, for example, the spinning wheel of an aged spinning woman), this proved too complicated for the cumbrous parish apparatus. Sight of the Elizabethan intention was not lost, though: it was clear that some other device must be tried. Most favoured was the workhouse, the most effective available method of regulating the poor until the complete breakdown of indoor relief in the 1790s. The creation of workhouse unions, especially Gilbert's Act 1782, further recognised that the parish was too confined a unit to organise pauper employment individually, and contracting the workhouse raised as many questions as it solved. With all the multiplicity of experiments, however, it proved impossible to employ the poor at a profit, and the universal application of the workhouse system in 1834 had deterrence, not profit, as its *raison d'être*.

Thus the parish, its officers and organisation, demonstrates real care, where its original population conditions obtained. The inadequacy of the autonomous and isolated administrative arrangements was most felt when responding to urban growth. It was to meet such challenges that parishes grouped into unions, and that the nineteenth century became a bureaucratic age. Utility and the public good necessarily came to replace local self-help.

5 Public Awareness

It was in the sphere of social politics that public opinion had a practical effect. Because administration was local, it was sensitive to the expression of opinion, and to a marked degree acted in accord with its dictate. Increasingly this was the case. At the one extremity, opinion held that poverty resulted from the organisation of society and that lack of material possessions implied a certain virtue; at the other, that pauperism was evidence of God's will, or of moral turpitude, involving idleness and profligacy. Both currents may be discerned in the years from 1660 to 1834, but it is worth noting that the poor themselves leave little or no record of what they thought: democratic movements were in abeyance from the Restoration to the nineteenth century.

The pauper was an unwanted part of the State heritage of the English Reformation. Monastic ideals of simple charity were not readily adopted by the new society, whose concern with a competitive economy became more apparent as the seventeenth century progressed. The 'cult of Independency' left the poor outside the aegis of both Church and monarchy. Private charity, flowing from the source of individual conscience, was less prolific from 1640 to 1660 (**27**), and the extra streak of hardness that seemed to enter public life in the Restoration Age, the tendency to oligarchy, further contributed to stemming the flow though it was far from drying up. For example, far from regulating the corn market in times of scarcity, in 1670 the import of corn was restricted until it had reached almost 80s a quarter, the infamous figure of the 1815 Corn Law, and in 1683 a permanent bounty on export was established.

The Puritan ethic had laid stress on the duty and rhythm of work —saints' days were anathema to a hard-headed business mentality— and the distinction between deserving and idle poor was sharply drawn by the entrepreneur Puritan, the more so as pauperism grew. As Professor Tawney pointed out (**4a**), the scepticism of the Restoration which 'saw in misfortune the punishment for sin', was later directed against the Speenhamland policy. The Church of England, muted and unsure of its identity, made no real contribution. Poverty verged on the criminal to the collective mind of the 'lusty plutocracy' of the Restoration, and severity found advocacy in the writings of the school of Political Arithmeticians, exemplified by Sir William Petty (**104**), who examined the problems of putting the poor to work in a series of pamphlets. Sir Matthew Hale (**97**) and Sir Josiah Child (**86**) attacked the Settlement Amendment for obstructing the mobility of labour, and argued, prophetically, for unions of parishes; so also did Richard Haines (**96**). In observing that 'honest tradesmen' could not find work, Hale came close to analysing that which was wrong, and such writers looked to the United Provinces to exemplify the potential profitability of idle hands. Petty had observed in 1662 that 'fewness of men is real poverty'. The philanthropist, Thomas Firmin (**94**), as an antidote to mere almsgiving, encouraged self-help by setting the poor to work in his enlightened linen manufactory, while Richard Dunning assigned the poor to contractors or undertakers, on pain of commitment to the House of Correction if they refused. Others took up the cry, and even the admirable Quaker, John Bellers, advocated a 'College of Industry' in 1695.

Such writings largely ignored the crux of the problem, that of the causes of unemployment which is a recurring spectre of modern commercial society, and which derive directly from it. The presence of this situation was the responsibility of society at large, but was not admitted by any contemporary writer, innocent of the study of sociology. John Locke, most influential among English political philosophers, had all too familiar an opinion of the condition of the poor, as resulting from 'a relaxation of discipline and corruption of manners' (**102**): suppression, especially of drinking, was his remedy. Thomas Alcock had even proposed the revival of sumptuary legislation (**81**).

Ironically, Locke's aim of closing 'superfluous brandy shops' was to be fulfilled by the War of the Spanish Succession, which resulted in the replacement of the offending French beverage by patriotic gin (for the horrifying social consequences of which see Chapter 10). Locke's proposals in the direction of severity bordered on making the pauper a slave, and included the device of the Labour Rate which was actually incorporated in the 1820s, yet they reflected political sentiment and at least offered the merit of change in an unacceptable situation.

The pen of Daniel Defoe had perhaps an even greater effect on public feeling; certainly it was more damaging, and he was right in condemning the naïvety of the hopes for making a profit from the labours of the poor. The effect was transitory. Mackworth's Bill of 1704 was killed, but the idea of 'setting the poor to work' lived on. John Cary's proposal for a workhouse for Bristol in 1695 (**85**) had actually resulted in legislation, and the success of the Authority (though not its profitability) helped the passing of further permissive legislation in 1723.

Public attitudes towards the new industrial proletariat remained uniformly harsh down to the middle years of the eighteenth century when, in the poised and pacific Age of Classicism, there occurred the development of humanitarian and philanthropic endeavour. The complacency of this epoch, of men such as Blackstone, Gibbon, and Burke, was challenged by those like Hogarth, Fielding and Smollett, who investigated the reality behind the classical façade. The philanthropists, Hanway, Coram, Oglethorpe and Howard, were men whose sensitivity to the suffering and needs of the unfortunate swung opinion and, moreover, resulted in the construction of practical memorials, of hospitals, prisons and schools. Compassion was equally sharply reflected in literature (see Bibliography). The new puritanism of Robert Nelson, Lady Elizabeth Hastings, the Wesleys, Cowper and Wilberforce, by stressing the charity of the New Testament, contributed to an easier climate of opinion. Satire, rather than arithmetic, was the weapon employed by Smollett and Fielding against the favouritism and tyranny of pauper administration. Tracts of the 1750s, of Massie, Joshua Tucker and John Scott, emphasised the rights and conditions of men, and dissatisfaction with workhouse practice helped the assertion of general sympathy for the poor: Gilbert's Act of 1783 was a sign not merely that public sentiment had changed, but that it bore consequences.

Such small benevolence as was implicit in Gilbert's Act responded to an apparently cyclical law by giving way once more to a rigorous phase of opinion. The new inspirational force was Utilitarian: its criteria, of the pursuit of happiness and self-interest, found a wide acceptance. Benthamite political economics required poor relief to be given to the able-bodied only in well-ordered workhouses, and in conditions inferior to those of the humblest labourer outside. 'The great discovery was left to the Utilitarian philosophers that relief was to be administered both to relieve and to deter' (**42**). The

21

philosophy was suited to industrial society, freeing labour by driving the manual worker into the labour pool. Cobbett's assertion that a pauper was only a very poor man was a cry in the wilderness, before the barren Utilitarian concept that lack of wealth was a crime and that the poor exhibited moral failings; it followed from a society which increasingly paid homage to mammon.

Yet again public opinion had shifted, and on this occasion its outcome was the Poor Law Amendment Act of 1834. Benthamite utility demanded efficiency, and state action established a new epoch of professionalism and supervision.

Part Two

ANALYSIS

6 The Poor and the Administration

Although the Poor Law derived from Elizabethan statute, the implied cohesive element of a strong executive was lacking during the period 1660–1834. It was administered by men whose responsibilities ceased at their parish boundaries, whose actions were in no way called to account, and whose increasing difficulties all too often failed to attract the attention of a myopic central government. Yet there were evolutionary changes, which, far from startling by their originality, heighten impressions of the gradualism of English social and political reactions to technological revolution. Successive governments were, however, pressed by widening public opinion to accept responsibility for public welfare, until Whigs and Peelites alike were persuaded by the most clamorous element, the Utilitarians, of the necessity of central control.

But more important than any conceptual initiative was the pressure of events. Thus changes were episodic and erratic, meeting by expediency the demands of novel situations. This was not an age of ideological awareness, and nowhere is it more apparent than in the history of the poor. The only pattern which can with certainty be discerned is that, as the problem intensified, so the effectiveness of the Tudor machinery declined.

The 1601 Act codified much previous Tudor legislation, and definitively brought the problem of poverty beneath state responsibility. A dual administrative principle was asserted, by which the parish was established as the unit, and the unit was under the central, and secular, supervision of the Privy Council. Its intentions were to differentiate the work-shy from the dutiful unemployed; to provide vocational education for the children of paupers; and to relieve those unable to work through age, sickness, or disability. Severe economic depression in the 1590s had, by swelling the ranks of the unemployed, forced the issue.

The fact of unemployment, which had been little experienced in static agrarian societies, was openly recognised by the provision and

25

management of stocks of commodities to set the poor on work. Poor children were to be bound out as apprentices, compulsorily until males reached the age of twenty-four, females until twenty-one, or marriage. The practical humanity of these measures was offset by the severity shown towards rogues, vagabonds and sturdy beggars. Begging was prohibited, and the vagabond, formerly dealt with under the Statute of 1576, was carefully defined (though he was no longer to be earmarked, the practice of ear-boring being dropped in this Act). He was to be whipped 'until his or her body be bloody' and be sent back to the place of birth (if unknown, to the place where he or she last dwelt). Furthermore, the whipping was to be repeated in each parish *en route*: the sturdy beggar well merited his alms. On his return, he was to be thrown into the common gaol or house of correction, which the justices were empowered to erect in each county and city, until he could be placed in service. 'Incorrigible and dangerous vagabonds' were to be banished or committed 'perpetually to the galleys of this realm'. Should they return, out of nostalgia, felons' deaths awaited them.

The desire to stamp out the 'professional poor' by punitive legislation went hand in hand with the encouragement, emphasised by Professor Jordan (**27**) of private endowment to hospitals, houses of correction and *maisons de Dieu* (almshouses).

This massive piece of state intervention was little tampered with up to 1660; it was briefly put to the test during the personal government of Charles I, the one real attempt at conciliar control. However, the social tradition of pauper relief and maintenance had been irreversibly established by the Elizabethan Poor Law, and it was this great construction which was in essence to remain, though modified in one direction, and intensified in another, until 1834.

Survival of the Law during the Interregnum nevertheless left scope for redefinition at the Restoration. Social disruption had taken place which affected stability and employment. The preamble to the Law of Settlement and Removal (1662), gives this view of the situation:

. . . People are not restrained from going from one parish to another, and therefore do endeavour to settle themselves in those parishes where there is the best stock, the largest commons or wastes to build cottages, and the most woods for them to burn and destroy, and when they have consumed it then to another parish, and at last become rogues and vagabonds, to the great discouragement of parishes to provide stock when it is liable to be devoured of strangers.

This impressionistic picture offered no background of fact, but the circumstances leading to the Act were real enough to justify some sort of remedial action: increasing population, economic upheaval resulting from war, and the absence of any compensating industrial boom.

The Act itself did little by way of providing remedy for the causes, and still less anything that was novel. Miss Leonard remarked that 1662 stereotyped a custom that had long been in existence in the towns' (28). Anyone who held 'any tenement under the yearly value of £10' or who was '*likely to be* chargeable to the parish' in the future, was to be removed to the last place of settlement [doc. 1]. Such removal had to be done, by application of a churchwarden or overseer to two magistrates for a warrant, within forty days. The tensions of many poor village immigrants may be imagined, as they awaited possible complaint, made probable by a reward (of 2s) offered to those 'informing or apprehending' for every rogue, vagabond, or sturdy beggar. These social outcasts were to be transported to the English plantations, and there 'disposed of in the usual way of servants', for up to seven years. Labour-hungry American colonists showed an eagerness to buy the service of English castaways. The City of London, as early as 1620, had disposed of 100 unwanted children in Virginia.

The main effect was to guard the parish against strangers with families. Those likely to become effective labourers were allowed a measured freedom by the interesting clause of 14 Car. II. c. 12, that a person moving for temporary work, such as harvesting, must carry a certificate from the minister of the parish, one of the churchwardens, and one of the overseers. This principle of 'certificating' was extended by legislation later in the century.

Settlement was rendered yet more difficult to obtain by the amendment of 1685, which effectively shortened the forty days' residence period by making it commence 'from time of Delivery of Notice in Writing of house of Abode, and Number of Family, to one of the Churchwardens or Overseers'. There was no longer the opportunity of quiet homesteading or surreptitious residence during the forty day period. It had been a small chance anyway, in rural parishes, but the odds were lengthened when Parliament further demanded, in 1693, that notice be given in writing, to be read in the parish church 'at the time of divine service'. The same Act defined other ways of gaining a settlement, which included serving an apprenticeship in the parish, being hired as a servant for one year, or paying parochial rates; while women gained settlement by marriage and children took that of their father until the age of seven. Illegitimate children were settled where they were 'dropped', which caused parishes to shunt pregnant girls along with undignified haste

The final parliamentary assertion regarding settlement gave legality to the practice of giving testimonials. This Act lifted the barrier against intruders, if they had a certificate 'under the Churchwardens Hands of any other Parish'—'the said other Parish to provide whenever they became chargeable'. By this proviso, parishioners were encouraged to seek work outside their own boundaries, and were egged on, where work was available, by the officers. The labour market thereby gained in flexibility, and agreements between the parishes modulated the discordant tone of mutual relations.

Such was the legislation concerning settlement. It has since provoked violent reactions. While the extreme views are incapable of reconciliation, there are dispassionate conclusions to be drawn. The law acted with irregular force. For able-bodied men, seeking work the settlement laws raised few problems. The law was much harsher to those men 'overburdened with children', to spinsters, and to women with children. Also, there was discrepancy between rural and industrial parishes, for in the latter (in textile regions especially) the young as well as the mature could be employed, and hence the family unit was more acceptable. Population did disperse and reform in the eighteenth century, and in any case the laws of settlement were not the only obstacles to progression from one vicinity to another. Walking was the only sure mode of travel available to the poor: in Cambridgeshire the majority of 'Certificate men' moved parish only within the county (**64**).

Settlement fundamentally altered the position of apprentices, who could now be put out to masters in other parishes. The system was beneficial both to the parish, obviously, and to the master, who either gained cheap labour or the fee he received for taking the children from the lap of the parish: the child was less likely to benefit from the transaction, as the common allusion to the runaway apprentice bears out [**doc. 28**].

The very practice of removal itself was a social degradation. To secure a removal was expensive enough, since the receiving parish frequently contested the case, entailing costly and absurd litigation. Once the legal claim had been determined, the pauper was carried, stage by stage, back to his, or her, place of settlement (facing a succession of whipping posts, if considered a vagrant), conveyed by constables who saw the intruders off their territory [**doc. 2**]. It is clear that the laws brought parishes into conflict, increased their insularity, and anchored the rural family, limpet-like, to the place of settlement.

Two other pieces of legislation bore on Poor Law administration. The first, the Game Act of 1671, has an oblique relevance, but illustrates well the political centre of gravity. Edible game was naturally a vital means of supplementing diet in the country, and its pursuit equally an object of apparent enjoyment. The landowners acted in Parliament to secure game rights, and continued to strengthen them during our period, a cruel restriction imposed by those for whom, after 1689, 'liberty' was to become a constitutional totem. There was, in the history of the game laws, an indication of whose liberty was to be preserved.

A final note of harshness was struck towards the close of the century, as part of the Act legalising testimonials. From 1 September 1697 those in receipt of allowance were forced to make public the badge of pauperism [**doc. 15**]. Refusal suspended relief payments at best; at worst the offender was committed to the house of correction 'there to be whipt and kept to Hard Labour' for any number of days up to twenty-one. Officials relieving non-badged paupers were themselves liable to a 20s fine. The cost of this fell on the parish, and at Bilston, Staffordshire, came to 1s 4d in 1703 'for setting ye badge upon 8 persons', but in 1726 had risen to 7s 7d, presumably due to the practice of casting the letters in brass. The stigma was hard to bear for many, especially those newly fallen on bad times. At Cheadle in 1703 'Elizabeth Salisbury, Mary Budworth, Hannah Scott and Ann Hinckley be taken out of the constant pay on their stubborn refusal to were the badge publicly'. Indignities were often less public: the poor in the West Bromwich workhouse, for two periods in the eighteenth century, wore around their necks iron collars, engraved with their names and that of the parish. An Act of 1810 ordered the discontinuation of the practice of badging the poor, which, understandably, had been found intolerable to many parishes.

A mass of pamphlets, but little in the way of action, excepting settlement legislation, was the response to the problem in the last phase of the seventeenth century. The solution of setting the poor to work, advocated by 43 Eliz. c. 2, was the most popular notion of the political arithmeticians, and particularly of the philosopher, John Locke, who was a distinguished servant of the Board of Trade, reconstituted in 1696 by William III. Vagrancy and the Poor Rate were the first subjects dealt with. Locke's proposed remedies were unequivocally based on the profitable employment of the poor, and were formally adopted by the Privy Council. Even with the King's active support, however, this came to nothing, though a Bill was introduced in 1705. The most important of several allied proposals— there were four Bills introduced in 1704 alone—was that of Sir Humphrey Mackworth. It incorporated elements of several of the leading economists, and received the applause of the House of Commons. Defoe's scathing opposition, however, turned the House of Lords to a policy of rejection, and setting the poor to useful work remained unblessed by Parliament for two decades.

This is not to say that there were no local initiatives. As Dorothy Marshall has pointed out, parliamentary action followed local experiment only after a cautious timelag (**13**). The workhouse solution had been widely advocated for many years when John Cary demonstrated its practicability in Bristol.

The basic concern with utilising the poor's labour recurred over and again. The Privy Council had striven to compel authorities to obtain stocks, and justices in the Quarter Sessions had from time to time condemned the slackness of officers in this regard, but the general failing was admitted. Apart from isolated attempts to arrange employment with manufacturers, useless on account of market fluctuation, and directives issuing from Sessions—as in the North Riding in 1693 to secure 'stock of flax, hemp, and wool and other ware and stuff ... towards setting on work of such as are able but cannot otherwise find employment' (**45**) there seemed no escaping the conclusion that the parish was too small a unit to supervise pauper employment. In consequence, Cary incorporated all the parishes within Bristol by an Act of Parliament in 1696. The 'Corporation of the Poor' made itself responsible for all the poor of the City, and opened a work house capable of employing them. Its initial success led to swift imitation, and workhouse schemes were implemented in Tiverton, Exeter Hereford, Colchester, Kingston and Shaftesbury, within two years.

In part, the results disappointed, because the workhouses were not a commercial success after the first few years, but on the other hand they did demonstrate sufficient deterrence to bring about general legislation. The Workhouse Act of 1723 permitted parishes to build and manage workhouses, making it 'lawful for two or more to unite in purchasing hiring or taking such house'. This gave parliamentary recognition to the main failing of the Elizabethan measures, the size of the administrative unit. Far more relevant, however, from the pauper's viewpoint, was the principle of the 'workhouse test', which was asserted in the Act. This made the pauper's right to relief dependent on his preparedness to enter the workhouse: 'In case any poor person shall refuse to be lodged kept or maintained in such house or houses, such poor person shall be put out of the book of those to receive collection.' The poor rate may have been curbed by the Act but it contributed nothing to giving profitable work to the poor, and established an institution which they found odious. Its purposes, to punish the idle, deter applicants for relief, house the infirm and provide work for the able-bodied, were effective, very nearly, in that order, and the numerous and evident abuses led to new legislation.

Sir Edward Knatchbull's Act of 1723, as well as establishing a test for relief and allowing for the combination of parishes, gave the parish licence to 'contract with churchwardens and overseers of any other parish for lodging the poor'. Contracts were made either for the payment of a lump sum or on a capitation basis, and provided yet more extensive grounds for criticism.

The degeneration of workhouse practice fostered opposition and it was not until 1756 that rural parishes attempted localised experiments in the Hundred Houses of Carlford and Colneis, Suffolk. Nothing substantial was achieved, however, until Gilbert's Act of 1782. Thomas Gilbert was zealous in amending the Poor Laws, and had pushed a Bill through the Commons in 1765 for grouping the parishes in large districts, such as Hundreds. As the preamble explained, the poor 'contract Habits of Idleness for want of finding some suitable Employment, whereby they gradually become vicious and dissolute, until at length they grow desperate in Wickedness, to the great Terror and frequent Injury of their Fellow Subjects, as well to their own utter Undoing'. The Heads of the Bill again proposed the remedy of purchasing 'a convenient Stock of Hemp, Wool, Cotton, Thread, Iron, Stone, Wood, Leather, or other Materials for the Employment of the Poor'. The measure was rejected in the

Upper House by 66 to 59, and the situation awaited future evidence. In 1774 Parliament attempted to obtain it, with Gilbert still a forceful figure, by obliging the Overseers to make returns relative to the state of the poor.

There was some logical basis, therefore, for the effective suspension of the 'workhouse test', which came in Gilbert's Act of 1782. Having worked energetically at the subject for many years, Gilbert introduced three Bills. The first two, amending the laws regulating houses of correction and enabling combinations of parishes, passed into law; the third, to reform Acts about vagrancy, miscarried. The Act was not obligatory, but any parish adopting it was not permitted to maintain or hire out the poor by contract, and the workhouse was reserved solely to those made indigent by old age, sickness, or infirmity. A visitor, 'respectable in character and Fortune', was to be appointed by the justices to superintend the poor house.

The clause allowing the infant poor to be put out at 'such weekly allowance as shall be agreed by the parish officers' had been anticipated by occasional experiments for two hundred years, and interestingly by the parish of St James, Westminster, in 1762. This was an atypical vestry, well organised and handling a manageable number of paupers. It was empowered to appoint twenty-one gentlemen as Governors and Directors of the Poor, in liaison with the churchwardens and overseers. These were authorised to make byelaws to care for their paupers. Children 'mouldering away in the workhouse' were placed 'after much search and great difficulty' with several cottagers on Wimbledon Common (**14**). The terms offered the nurses were generous enough at 3*s* per week per child, and additionally included a system of bonus payments, such as '5*s* for every child recovering from hooping cough or the measles', and one guinea for every child living a year if sick or infirm, or under twelve months old. The nurse was discontinued if two children died within a year. This was the system incorporated in the general Act, and there was the additional humane safeguard that 'nothing . . . shall give any power to separate any child or children, under the age of seven years, from his, or her, or their parent or parents, without the consent of such parent or parents'. The enlightened intention of this clause was out of context with the characteristic treatment of the 'idle and disorderly, able and unwilling' who were to be prosecuted and punished as under George II. 17, which had recodified, for the last time of many, before 1822, the Elizabethan Vagrancy Statutes

Gilbert's Act, thoroughly researched and skilfully drafted, encouraged parishes to group together into unions, and the professional guardian was expected to replace the temporary rule of casual and corrupt overseers. Its most important stress was laid on the new role of workhouses as providing a home for the impotent poor: the able-bodied were to exist on dole payments, together with the work which overseers were instructed to provide extramurally, even to the extent of making up any deficiency in earnings by the so-called 'extra-ordinary clause'. By these provisions, the Act of 1723 was condemned and rejected.

That, at least, was the verdict of Parliament; but the will of Parliament was unenforceable. Only 924 parishes had combined to form a mere 67 unions by 1830. These were not specially well regulated and there is basis for assuming that those parishes which did adopt the Gilbertian idea did so for mainly financial considerations.

Consistent with the narrow application of the Gilbert union workhouse was the decline in the condition of the labouring poor. The year 1783 concluded the exhausting American War and inaugurated a hazardous, and all-too-familiar, postwar depression, intensified by industrial reorganisation and poor harvests. The reopening of Anglo-French hostilities in 1793 further accelerated price rises, which were diminishing the value of labouring wages. Riots followed in the spring and summer of 1795, and though they had little political content, their appearance alarmed simply by the association of ideas with revolutionary France. They were, in fact, mainly hunger riots, with women (but beware the March of the Women!) well to the fore in seizing flour and other foodstuffs, which they distributed on their own terms. Two mills were destroyed by rioters in Devonshire, though 'from the great number of petticoats, it is generally supposed that several men were dressed in female attire'. A variety of placebos, most famously represented by Speenhamland, were prescribed to alleviate the consequential fear and compassion.

Speenhamland was no system, though it was extensively applied throughout the southern counties, and found its way to all areas except Northumberland. As the first decision to lay down a scale of relief according to the price of bread and the size of the family, it gave a positive lead for the provision of outdoor relief. Moreover, it was realistically tied to basic necessity and showed benevolent intent. The Berkshire magistrates met at 'ten o'clock in the forenoon' on

6 May 1795, at the Pelican Inn in Speen. They numbered twenty, including seven clergymen, and accepted unanimously the resolution that 'the present state of the Poor does require further assistance than has generally been given them'. It was determined to regulate the wages of day labourers by calculating aid on the following basis: that when the 'Gallon Loaf of second Flour, weight 8 lbs 11 ozs' cost 1s, every 'poor and industrious Man' should receive 3s per week allowance for himself, and 1s 6d for the support of his wife and each member of his family. When the price rose to 1s 4d, the labourer's allowance was to increase to 4s for his own needs, plus 1s 10d for 'every other of his family'. 'And so in proportion as the price of bread rises or falls (that is to say) 3d to the man and 1d to every other of the family on every penny which the loaf rises above a shilling.' The labourer's need was therefore assessed at three gallon loaves a week, twice that of his dependents.

There had been earlier attempts to regulate allowances, as at the Oxford Quarter Sessions in January 1795, and the widespread adoption of Speenhamland can only be accounted for by the announcement of a specific and applicable scale. Parliament swiftly gave authority for the donation of outdoor relief to persons in distress (55 Geo. III c. 137), and it rapidly gained grateful acceptance, even infiltrating weaving and manufacturing districts. That it gave rise to embittered class relations is unchallengeable, but at least it afforded labourers a minimum level of subsistence in lieu of a minimum wage [**doc. 12**].

This last proposal emanated from Samuel Whitbread, and was another in the line of parliamentary initiatives which promised much, only to disappoint. An Elizabethan Act of 1563 had empowered the justices to fix maximum wage rates, and it was this which Whitbread, with the support of Sheridan and Grey, and the Members for Suffolk, sought to destroy. Fox spoke in favour at the first reading, but by the second, on 12 February 1796, an opposition had been mustered. Pitt alone was adversary enough: he argued that the poor were supported by 'beneficence never surpassed at any period' and saw remedy in the 'free circulation of labour', in restoring the 'original purity' of the Poor Laws, and in encouraging Friendly Societies to take over the public burden of pauper maintenance. Pitt's authority was overwhelming, and it killed the Bill without a second reading.

But Pitt had committed himself to introducing a Bill of his own.

He considered that Whitbread distorted the plight of the poor, and he accordingly went about drawing up his own proposals, mixing wages supplementation with crude provisions for old age pensions and schools of industry. These were circulated in the country, and provoked much interested comment [**doc. 13**]. Of particular note was his cow-money proposal: '. . . by the Advance of Money for purchasing a Cow or other Animal yielding Profit, . . . it shall be lawful to order the Payment of such Money in Advance as will be necessary for the Purchase of such Cow . . . out of the Rates'. This at least recognised that ruin ought to be averted, not cured, but the Bill as a whole lacked unity, and the clause to pay wages out of rates would have resulted in something akin to Speenhamland. Bentham's 'corroding sarcasm' led informed criticism, and this 'strange document' was curiously introduced with no defender but the Prime Minister himself, making for a 'conversation' rather than a debate. It is tempting to infer that Pitt's motive was to destroy Whitbread's measure by criminal adoption, yet it is clear that he devoted much time to the matter. Other problems were weighing on his mind, and his inexperience of the condition of the poor—the squalor in which they lived was a revelation to him, when pointed out by his private secretary when he was staying at Halstead in Essex—could explain his diffidence. Or it may simply be that the complexity of this problem only became apparent on close acquaintance, and that he had been deluded by apparently facile solutions.

Intuition did not always mislead Pitt, as he rightly pressed—admittedly with the encouragement of his economics mentor, Adam Smith—for a 'radical amendment' of the laws of settlement, and he was the power behind Sir William Young's Act (35 Geo. III c. 101). This followed a number of pamphlets advising on its efficacy and some parliamentary ventures. The overseers could, from 1662, remove those liable to become chargeable, but this practice was mollified by the growth of certificating, and in 1784 was extended to sailors, soldiers, and their families. In 1793 this privilege of avoiding rejection on suspicion was extended to members of registered Friendly Societies. Young had proposed reform in the Commons in 1788, and succeeded in 1795 in preventing removal until a person became actually chargeable. The certificate method had not kept pace with growing demand for industrial labour, now under the additional strain of war, and Young's reform facilitated labour mobility, while causing little complaint from parishes in a period of exceptional demand for the produce of industry. The Act also laid down that no sick or infirm person regarded as unfit to travel by the justices was to come under a removal order, a humane provision extended to the family of the sick in 1809.

By the Act, certificates were rendered unnecessary, but temporary distress—markedly on the increase—more than accounted for the continued high incidence of removal. A Bill, introduced by Mr Baker and supported by Pitt, sought to deal with victims of transient recession, a key factor in Pitt's own Bill. The propositions were rejected as oppressive to the landed interest and as a 'premium for idleness and extravagance'. The voting figures, 30 to 23, demonstrate both apathy and the ease of organising pressure interests which, more than legislation, was the function of the unreformed Parliament.

With Pitt's promise to restore the Poor Law to its pristine benevolence broken, Whitbread made a second attempt to press his views on the House in 1800. Pitt again spoke against passing a general law. Whitbread's argument, following five years' experience of Speenhamland practice, that the poor should not depend on charity for subsistence, was unanswerable, but was not supported by a powerful enough grouping, as the Foxites had gone to ground. The Legal Minimum Wage project was finally shelved, for two decades, after Whitbread had made a last unsuccessful bid in 1807.

Speenhamland and statutory minimum wages were not the only proposals to make up the disparity between income and expenditure, so wide in the worst periods of 1795–96, and 1799–1800. What the Hammonds (**17**) described as 'an infinite vista of kitchen reform' persuaded reformers that the poor could survive on less costly food, if only menus were more scientifically planned [**doc. 14**]. Thomas Bernard, for example, put his faith in Count Rumford's demonstration of food and fuel economy, and pursued it through his Society for Bettering the Condition and Increasing the Comforts of the Poor. The Reports of the Society contained bizarre suggestions such as 'Of the Manner and Expence of Making Stewed Ox's Head for the Poor'. Food charities flourished in the bad years, and soup was offered at twenty-two different establishments in the Metropolis in 1799–1800, supported by £10,000 from London philanthropists. 'Though as an agency of social betterment it never justified the faith of Bernard, Colquhoun, and its other sponsors' (**37**), the soup kitchen had come to stay. It is perhaps sobering to realise that they are still organised.

Eden's Report of 1797 (**92**) showed the value of cheap cereals, in comparing the oatmeal/barley/rye-consuming North with the wheaten South. His findings were endorsed by correspondence in the *Annals of Agriculture* (**109**), which claimed that the poor would eat only the finest bread. Fox pointed to the weakness of this objection in the Commons debate on corn prices in November 1795. Acknowledging that mixed bread tasted 'highly pleasant' and doubtless was 'exceedingly wholesome', it nevertheless, he said, 'ought to be recollected how very small a part the article of bread forms of the provisions consumed by the more opulent members of the community. To the poor it constitutes the chief, if not the sole article of subsistence.' Underlying factors not always taken into account were also made clear by Eden's figures of milk consumption, which supplemented and flavoured oatmeal. The growth of tea drinking was hastened by milk shortage, and was condemned by moralists and dietitians alike. It was, as Davies wrote, 'not the cause, but the consequence, of the distress of the poor' (**89**).

Diets were often unadopted due to the shortage of fuel. Commons enclosure had reduced the possibility of fuel-gathering, and nourishing soups could not be prepared without fire. Many of the recipes were, of course, for communal sustenance, and Arthur Young's is characteristic and worth quoting.

To each copper, containing thirty gallons, I put one sheep of from 25 lbs. to 30 lbs., a peck of potatoes, half a peck of onions, a peck of carrots, a peck of turnips, half a peck of pease, 6 lbs. of rice, and it made most excellent soup, which the poor relished exceedingly, and the outsetters of the parish, who lived five miles off, came for it very readily (**107**).

For the practical Young, the substitution of rice, soup and oat flour, for wheat and money, was the 'remedy of all evils'. He would have needed to add fuel to make the project workable, and to have overcome the understandable prejudice of the poor themselves who, incomprehensibly to their pastry-fed betters, clung to dietary conservatism [**doc. 14**].

Outdoor relief, either graduated under Speenhamland, or arbitrarily ladled out by soup-kitchens, lasted down to the end of the period. The emotions engendered by the French Revolution and the ensuing wars produced a political log-jam which served also to hold up social progress, making extreme solutions wait on the reformed parliament.

37

Reform, however, had on its side the most vital of stimulants, money. The expense of the Poor Law, especially in the South, became the major concern as costs escalated to the maximum figure of almost £8 million in 1817. This sort of statistic gained credence for the reforming programme in the postwar years. But it was a slow process, as parliamentary and local forces ignored drastic remedy, standing fast beside a known expedient. It was a high price to ask from the ratepayers, but they were prepared to meet it, as a guarantee against Jacobin excesses. The period has been described as an age of misplaced generosity: it could perhaps better be considered one of calculated self-preservation.

Information from the overseers was requested by an Act of 1803, instigated by the able Pittite, George Rose, who had already, in 1793 and 1795, obtained the passage of two Acts for the protection and regulation of Benefit Clubs, affecting the laws of settlement. The voluminous data submitted was probably obtained from the payment of fees for the officers who gave evidence of workhouse profits, or rather their absence. A complex number of problems was investigated, and the information was diligently tabulated by John Rickman and Thomas Poole. More statistics continued to be compiled by select committees of the House of Commons from 1817 onwards, but with insubstantial consequences. The Sturges-Bourne Act of 1819 merely altered the franchise and voting methods of the Open Vestry (in which any parishioner paying a few shillings per annum in poor relief could participate). Legislation with regard to vestries was advanced by Hobhouse's Act of 1831, 'the first instalment of the legislative revolution by which English local government has been placed on a representative basis' (**73**). This enabled those parishes still ruled by Select Vestries to elect their vestrymen, and its effect was the disappearance of the Select Vestry, as at Marylebone and St Pancras.

For decades there had been academic criticism of the Poor Laws, and the allowance system was weighing so heavily that even reactionary minds searched reform programmes, if only in the hope of finding financial relief. Adam Smith, though favouring high wages, was enrolled in the argument against regulation and control, while the offensive of Malthus, 'dependent poverty ought to be held disgraceful', was unchallenged by those paying the price of dependence. Malthus adapted French physiocratic views about the peasant who, in Turgot's words, 'ne gagne que sa vie', to deliver the conundrum that severity was benevolence, since the relief of poverty led to its increase. For Malthus, the law of population ruled; for Ricardo, a rigid 'iron law of wages' provided jurisdiction (**105**). The synthesis of their writings, as understood by the politically articulate class, was that wages depended inexorably on capital and the size of population. Perhaps the most important harbinger of nineteenth century reform was Jeremy Bentham, who insisted that parochial action could have no part in an efficient industrial complex. These figures, with their influential followings, gave the rudimentary notions of Thomas Paine, of old age pensions, maternity benefits, and free and compulsory education, an appearance of crudity. Paine was a prophet with a longer vision: the provisions of 1834 depended on the vision of others, whose 'brutal surgery' has generally been considered necessary to the time and the problem.

However, this narrative does not allow too great an emphasis on the theorists, even if they merit it. More relevant was the negative view of the ratepayers, the squirearchy and clergy. Distress after 1793 had one certain result, the increase of the poor rates, which in the southern counties, according to Chambers and Mingay (**7**) rose in the 1820s to 20s an acre, as much as the land was worth in rents. These ratepayers suspected a malign connection between outdoor relief, idleness, large families, unemployment and high poor rates. The revisionist view of Mark Blaug (**56**), that evidence of the 'corrupting influence of lavish relief' had little validity, is a convincing historical judgement, but also serves to re-emphasise the prejudice of contemporary public opinion.

Their demand for fundamental alteration was concerted in recognising the seemingly obvious, that the allowance system had encouraged pauperism to spread. Their demands were given weight by the agricultural disturbances of 1830. These riots were worst where Speenhamland was strongest rooted, and the incendiarism and violence against threshing machinery in the southern counties undoubtedly contributed to attitudes represented in the Report of the Commissioners.

The Whig government, elected on a reform ticket, decided on intervention, and a Royal Commission was appointed in 1832 to report on the Administration and Operation of the Poor Laws. It included two bishops, of London and Chester, Sturges Bourne, Frankland Lewis, and Nassau Senior. The voice of the poor was unrepresented and there were few discordant voices to be heard in the chorus of complaint. The justices and overseers, the squires and parsons, spoke of the unjust and impolitic nature of the rate in aid of wages, and the Commissioners were equally decisive in their recommendations to Parliament.

The resultant Poor Law Amendment Act of 1834 (4 & 5 Will. IV c. 76) was different in kind and degree from the measures so far outlined. Benthamite political economy determined the Act's revolutionary premise, that poor relief should be available to the able-bodied poor only in conditions deliberately ordered to be inferior to those of the worst-paid independent labourer. This was the old Workhouse Test writ large, but in a most austere form. It rejected Malthusianism by aiming to restore the productive capacity of the worker, and to risk the consequences.

The Act was an 'administrative schedule', and its terms were to be compulsorily implemented. Those terms were that the parishes were grouped together in unions, each under a Board of Guardians, elected on a rate-paying franchise. The guardians were to be controlled by a new body, the Poor Law Commission, whose first Secretary was Chadwick, the highly effective hot-gospeller of Benthamism. The Commissioners were to enjoy a wide degree of discretion with regard to policy, but they were under ministerial control, and were not to sit in Parliament, so avoiding the eighteenth century stigma of jobbery. By these means, chaos was ordered, benevolence terminated.

This legislation met contemporary needs with contemporary philosophy, and is not to be condemned for that. Indeed, it is not intended to condemn the effects at all. But the assumption which was explicit in its proposals was that the Old Poor Law was a complete failure, and outdoor relief its most damaging aspect. Essentially, it had ceased to be a system long before 1834, but as a device for dealing with surplus labour in an expanding economy it was not ineffective—at least, there were no statistics to prove the contrary in the Commissioners' Report—nor was it unenlightened, surely a consideration when viewed from the comfortable premises of a society structured to provide, as of right, the basic necessities of life. Change there had to be, though, for while compromise can operate satisfactorily in a static social environment, it rarely succeeds in a dynamic situation.

7 The Circumstances of Poverty

HOUSING CONDITIONS

The debate on the material effects of industrialism is as yet unresolved, and centres most subtly on whether the acknowledged increase of commodities was distributed to all sections of society. The costs of food, drink, and housing were little affected by technical developments anyway, and the increasing population constantly threatened increasing consumption [**doc. 21**]. Household possessions altered little from their eighteenth century appearance [**doc. 23**]. But it must be conceded that without technological advances, people would have been unable to congregate satisfactorily in conurbations. Pestilence may, as the parasitologists inform us, have been dispelled by the humanitarian flea of the brown Hanoverian rat: its continued control demanded the iron pipe to duct water, and Cornelius Whitehouse's invention of 1825 enabled vast numbers to inhabit towns, in sanitary isolation one from the other. The iron pipe itself, however, was a product of the Industrial Revolution, and it is this type of chicken and egg situation which produces so many *non sequiturs* from economic historians.

The rural cottager was no stranger to the evils of bad housing, but their nature owed much to the locality. The presence, or otherwise, of natural building materials often made the difference between the appearance of affluence and squalor. Cotswold cottagers were able to build with local limestone, while the poor of Bridgnorth carved troglodytic homes in the sandstone cliffs. There is, of course, a dearth of hard evidence, since the poor's dwellings have not survived; the standard cottage described in contemporary accounts had one room upstairs, often serving as a hayloft. Roofing was most commonly in thatch or tiles (Welsh slate waited on the transport revolution for its ubiquitous employment). The cold Midlands clays furnished a building material which Cobbett observed in Leicestershire: 'Look at the miserable sheds in which the labourers reside!

41

Look at these hovels, made of mud and straw; bits of glass, or of old off-cast windows, without frames or hinges frequently, but merely stuck in the mud wall . . . the floor of pebble, broken brick, or of the bare ground'. In Lancashire, in 1815, cottages built of the ancient method of 'clot and clay' gave a 'hovel-like appearance far from agreeable'. Single room huts are reported in all regions from East Anglia to Cumberland and Northumberland. In the latter, it was reported as late as 1850 that cows and pigs lodged under the same roof as humans, the cowhouse being divided only by 'a slight partition wall' (**9**). Turf huts were erected on commons by squatters, and remained where tolerated. Poor Law officials, however, frequently had these pulled down or refused their miserable owners relief on the ground of their being property owners.

None of this is at all startling: where 'improvement' had yet to reach agrarian areas, expectations would be of conditions relating to the earliest settlements. What, though, was the effect of agrarian change, of enclosure? Contemporaries tended to less equivocation than historical commentators, and spoke freely of the poor being driven from the land (**109**). A parliamentary Act of 1757 seemed to give away the case by directing commissioners for enclosures to pay the poor law authorities compensation 'to be applied towards the relief of the poor in the parish or township where . . . wastes woods and pastures had been enclosed'. A tract of ground was sometimes kept for the use of the poor, or else they were awarded small lots for grazing flocks. But such compensation was seldom granted; plots were rarely set aside.

Enclosures, by engrossing farms, caused homelessness; the Poor Law aggravated the condition by making it the concern of every landlord to discourage labourers' cottages or small farms which might shelter a potential pauper [**doc. 24**]. The Elizabethan Law of 1597 which required every cottage to have four acres of land attached but had long been obsolete was repealed in 1775. The spaciousness which it foresaw had given way by 1800 to overcrowding and sanitary neglect—'cottages are in general the habitations of labourers, who all swarm with children; many have double, treble, and even quadruple families' (**110**).

The urban housing of the poor was even more strongly affected by eighteenth century economic rationalisation than that of the countryside. Accelerated pressure on urban space and materials caused an explosive building boom in which speculation yielded up

42

to 25 per cent return on capital investment. The jerry-builders who took advantage of such market conditions have received repetitive condemnation, though perhaps Professor Ashton's laconic refusal to apportion blame, on the ground that they were the only people to do the building, is worth bearing in mind (1). The system was not geared to accommodate the armies of the proletariat, which encamped in South Wales, the Black Country, the Potteries, Lancashire. The answers to urban growth, it should be remembered, continue to elude town planners.

The only remedies available were inadequate. Building materials were in short supply, and fission was the most effective means of architectural reproduction. Houses subdivided suddenly, to reveal cellars and garrets, additional sheds, rooms split by partition. The process was spontaneous, often in response to the arrival of the immigrants, whose poignant plight was especially represented among the Irish—a people who failed to industrialise, and emigrated or expired, innocent of whether industrialism was a triumph or disaster. The town houses themselves were of sounder construction, on the whole, than those ephemeral dwellings of mud, wattle, and moistened clay, left behind in Merrie England. But the buildings lacked water and sanitation, and were pressed together in rows, ultimately back-to-back.

Miss George (14) has graphically described the housing of the London poor in the eighteenth century, stressing that the one-room tenement was common, but not representative. London, like other English cities, and unlike European counterparts, grew outwards, and the sprawling, land-consuming terraces have become the visually hideous norm. London's growth was particularly influenced by restrictions on new building in the city. As poor people multiplied, and clamoured for house-room, labyrinthine courts and alleyways grew up behind main thoroughfares, attractive to rats and criminals alike.

What buildings there were inclined to impermanence; flimsy materials were used where a threat of demolition for breach of a bye-law existed. Subject to taxation and expensive, bricks were made from a mixture of 'the slop of the streets, ashes, scavengers' dirt, and everything that will make the brick earth or clay go as far as possible'. Dr Johnson remarked, irresistibly, that London was a place where 'falling houses thunder on your head'.

The squalid and filthy districts of London in which the poor jostled were worsened by the poor law policy of strict settlement within tiny parishes. There was no escape, without forfeiture of relief, from an urban environment which included, for those within nasal range of the Fleet Ditch, the offal from tripe dressers, sausage makers and catgut spinners, in addition to the more universal effluvia carried away in innumerable open sewers.

Free construction was also inhibited by the Window Tax, the original enforcement of which in 1696 was stiffened repeatedly, and not repealed until 1851. Houses not rated to the Church and the poor, on account of poverty, were exempted, but this did not apply to tenements and it became, after the 1710 increase, 'universal practice to stop up lights', with well-understood effects on the health of the inhabitants.

As elsewhere, the filthiest and poorest parts of London were occupied by the Irish. The rookery of St Giles contained one house in which each adult paid 3*d* a night, and reports gave evidence of forty people to a cellar, of accommodation shared with pigs and asses, and of cellars or garrets which could be rented at a shilling. By the mid-1830s, when housing conditions had become a recognised evil 15 per cent of Liverpool's population lived in cellars: the figure for Manchester was 11·75 per cent. The overcrowding of these places, and of Leeds, Preston, Bolton, and Bradford, the need for proximity to the place of work in the shanks's pony era, and the increasing use of houses for industrial occupations, made for a sorry environment. Primitive sanitation was unresponsive to the mild suggestions of the Court Leet of Manchester, which sought to persuade householders to empty barrels of excrement into the Irwell, at night, and discreetly.

The old were often housed in almshouses [**doc. 16**]. Increasing longevity made the aged a more specialised factor, and almshouses along with the smallest of the village cottages, attempted to deal with a need which now soon outgrew such small-scale remedy. They possess particular architectural interest from being founded by the gentry, 'not members of the classes which maintained the vernacular tradition' (**3**). Their elaborate façades continue to distinguish many an urban scene. But when the parish officers built for the old, the cheapest traditional methods sufficed. Towns had need of slow, calculated development, and no one had time to townscape, so that aesthetic sensibility was ignored in the stampede 'there was no urban Capability Brown'. The mud hovels of the countryside have disappeared from our view, but the industrial setting remains, and the haphazard agglomeration of urban housing, the melancholy ruin of industrial scenery, recalls the suddenness with which the social consequences of industrialism overtook the later part of our period. Had the authorities received warning of the approach of the homeless; had they possessed a blueprint to employ when they arrived; had they possessed the power to effect it: such considerations were as little pertinent as to the petrified citizens of Pompeii.

APPRENTICESHIP AND CHILD-LABOUR

Apprenticeship was the common experience of pauper children. The 1562–63 Statute of Artificers laid down the terms of a compulsory seven years under indentures of apprenticeship, and the provision of a trade was the laudable original intention of the Elizabethan Poor Law. As in so many cases, the intention was father to the abuse. Parishes which had as their legal wards the children of the poor, illegitimate children, and foundlings, had as part of their responsibilities to arrange their careers. The choices were limited, though opportunities altered as the period developed an industrial economy, but the authorities had two real alternatives: either they could bind the child within the parish at no initial cost, or use parish funds to place the child outside the parish, boys until twenty-four, girls until twenty-one or marriage [**doc. 27**]. The former was applied more in rural parishes, where farmers could make use of a juvenile labour force. The children bound outside their own parishes were normally from towns, and owed their plight in some measure to the settlement laws, for the procedure was that once a child had been bound over for the statutory forty days' residence, the new master's settlement was adopted: wardship was transferred. And since the authority of the new masters was bought by cash, exploitation was incited.

The notion of child-labour was considerably older than the Industrial Revolution: 'apprenticeship goes back to the flint-chippers' (**9**). But the regulations which contained the training of the young within limits broke down under the inexorable power of economic growth. The gilds, supervising their crafts in the old corporate towns, had no place in the new centres of population, and Manchester and Birmingham raised no smoke-stacks in honour of a regulative labour organisation.

45

Child-labour fell into two principal categories, apprentice and free labour. Pauper children were apprenticed from the beginning of the period, mainly in those trades which held little attraction, and still less prospects of advancement; working as stable-boys, chimney-sweeping, catgut-spinning—'a very mean, nasty, and stinking trade' —and, in the case of girls, to 'the art of housewifery', a euphemism for drudgery, or 'the literal slavery of milk-selling'; or worse. To a degree, they caused overstocking in some trades (the example of Nottingham stocking-weavers in the 1740s is often given) but the suggestion that apprentices were *only* put to trades which were already semi-pauperised, is an extreme view.

The amount of the premium was as infinitely varied as the nature of the work. A weaver or shoemaker might be paid £5 for taking a pauper child off the hands of the parish, an attractive incentive, whereas a chimney-sweep actually paid for his so-called apprentices, who were thus virtually sold into slavery. The runaway apprentice became part of the English scene, with rewards offered for recapture [**doc. 28**].

Quarter Sessions records and the reports of the Old Bailey testify to widespread violation. Ill-treatment under indentures caused many children to be hanged or transported, and complaints of the early eighteenth century reflected these melancholy records:

> . . . to apprentice poor children, to no matter what master, provided he lives out of the parish . . . [who] may be a tiger in cruelty, he may beat strip naked, starve or do what he will to the poor innocent lad . . . the greatest part of those who now take poor apprentices are the most indigent and dishonest, in a word, the very dregs of the poor of England. (*Enquiry into the Manners of the Poor*, 1738.)

All sorts of malpractices were possible, from hiring of the children to pressing them into the Royal Navy—a common habit of watermen, who then took their pay and prize-money. Masters hoped that the work value would exceed that of board and lodging, and parish assumptions were similarly mercenary: St Pancras Open Vestry ordered in 1722 that William Lucas be boarded out 'to what person or business . . . most proper, and to make as cheap a bargain for putting him out as he can'.

In the second half of the eighteenth century, parishes began to move tentatively in the direction of reform, an aspect of the new

humanitarianism. Industrial education lost some of its vogue for
the reformers, among whom Mrs Cappe provides an interesting
example. She attacked the apprenticing of girls from charity schools
on the ground that educational advantages were squandered by the
practice. With the Gray Coat School in York particularly in mind,
she averred that some of the girls had been 'seduced by masters',
that 'the health of others . . . had been completely ruined by ill-
usage'. She advocated finding places for wages, instead of apprenticeship for food and clothing, and the application of this system bore
good results. But the greatest friend of the apprentices was Jonas
Hanway, and he secured some tightening of masters' obligations,
increasing the premiums to be paid, and making them fall in two
instalments.

Yet at the very time when the dangers of apprenticeship were
exciting public concern, new circumstances were arising which were
to extend the exploitation of the infant poor. The factory system,
which embodied these new evils, was not entirely new, and children
had been sent to the cloth mills of the South-West, and the silk mills
of Derby, for years before. William Hutton (**100**) wrote of such
apprenticeship, describing his unhappy prospects as leading ultimately only to the workhouse; 'they all go there when they cannot
see to work'. But the machine, that wayward blessing, was itself
growing, even while it still needed an aquatic setting to function,
away from the population centres. The mill-owners were desperate
for a labour force which, by ironic coincidence, was made available
due to philanthropic effort. Hanway had had cause for complaint
in the 1750s and 1760s that few pauper children lived to be apprenticed, and by his Act of 1767 had 'caused a deficiency of 2,100 burials
a year' [**doc. 31**]. These survivors, the weakest, went to the new
mills of Lancashire, Derbyshire and Nottinghamshire: one Manchester manufacturer even agreed to take one idiot child with every batch
of twenty. The children were carted away to work for no reward
other than food and clothes, for up to fifteen hours a day in a Satanic
mill, lodged in unsegregated prentice houses. Even for Professor
Ashton (**1**) their story is 'a depressing one': for the Hammonds (**17**)
it was 'at best . . . monotonous toil, at worst . . . a hell of human
cruelty'. Of all the annals of the poor, the compulsory apprenticeship of children in distant textile mills is surely among the most
pathetic.

Not all mills offered a prospect of unmitigated misery. Smalley's

Mill at Holywell, Flintshire, accommodated 300 boys and girls in separate houses, 'whitewashed twice a year and fumigated three times a week with tobacco smoke', employed a surgeon, and sent the children to Sunday School (it was not elsewhere uncommon to work seven days a week). And Samuel Oldknow of Mellor, near Stockport, provided amply for the children who arrived from Clerkenwell and the Duke of York's Orphanage in Chelsea: 'No one had owt to complain of at Mellor' (**9**). Parishes which were considerate to their wards, such as St James, Westminster, and the carefully regulated Foundling Hospital, sent their children north.

The gulf which stood between educational and labouring apprenticeship had always been wide: it now became unbridgeable. The children were taught nothing to give hope of escape from the machine, and the remedies of 1747 and 1792, which allowed appeal by apprentices and fixed fines if successful, had little practical value. When employer and magistrate were the same person, protest was more than pointless; it was likely to provoke further victimisation. Peel's Act of 1802, the first of a long series of nineteenth-century Factory Acts, failed for want of an inspectorate, and the practice of transporting apprentices fell into disuse less due to the philanthropic than to the economic impulse. Steam power was emancipating the machine, and the demand for resident child-labour dropped as the factory system became urbanised; poor children then crowded the doors, their parents, 'the worst of taskmasters', anxious for employment. In 1816 the radius within which children might be apprenticed was limited to forty miles, and the 'carts ceased to dump their living freights at the mill-doors'.

The second, free labour, category of working children, inherited some of the protective instincts of the reformers, as regard for apprentice conditions developed into a condemnation of child-labour as such. Young children had been early put to work in the domestic system. It was productive of income, and prevented sinful idleness. When a handloom weaver could earn no more than 6s 6d a week, the additional bonus of children's earnings became a necessity. It was enforced, if not by the parents, then by the poor law officials who withheld relief from those who had employable children. The children started their working life at the age of six or seven, sometimes as early as three, according to Robert Owen's evidence to Sadler's Committee, which heard a woeful list of case histories [**doc. 29**]. Yet all the employers, with the exception of Owen and Peel, maintained that the children were not overworked. Parliamentary action up to the great Althorp Act of 1833 was negated by inadequate enforcement, and in any case applied only to cotton mills.

The scandalous treatment of children who worked underground lacerated consciences when their treatment was eventually exposed by Shaftesbury in 1842. Children under ten were employed as trappers, opening and closing the draught doors essential for ventilation, sitting in a hole at the side of the door for stretches of twelve hours, and in complete darkness. Alternatively, they became fillers of trucks, or 'pushers' or 'hurriers', conveying the coal to the foot of the shaft. The naked, girdled young girl, dragging a coal truck behind her, is perhaps the most evocative illustration of the whole period of child-labour. There was, of course, regional variation in conditions—South Staffordshire, for example, did not employ women or girls—but those who suffered most were generally parish children from the workhouses, who were 'made to go where other men will not let their own children go'.

Infant employment in mines and factories had the support of powerful interest groups, and pressure of economic circumstances counted for more than people; this much is comprehensible. But the failure of authority to prevent the ill-usage of infants as chimney sweeps defies credulity. Unknown on the Continent, this monstrous abuse was justified by the contemporary taste for ornate chimneys. Not that all chimneys swept were of a wide girth. Amazingly, human beings, naked and very tiny, groped up flues seven inches square: for boys of seven to mount with ease, a foot square was the necessary dimension. Protection was intended by Hanway's Act of 1788, but this was a classic instance of the inoperability of eighteenth-century regulative law. The numbers engaged in the trade are unobtainable. The benevolent master-sweep, David Porter, who fed his apprentices, according to Sir Thomas Bernard, on 'boiled mutton and rice pudding', estimated 200 sweeps and 2,000 apprentices. The poorest of parents could bind their children to a sweep, and younger than in any other occupation. Indeed, the younger the child, the better the price, and parents traded their offspring into apprenticed slavery at two or three years of age.

The conditions of work were unspeakable [**doc. 30**]. The prospective sweep had first to be inured to hardship; to overcome his fears of the dark, suffocating horizontal flues, of being burnt. He was kept aloft by beatings, by straw fires insufficiently fierce to kill him (he was valuable property), and by pins stuck in his feet. Physically, too, he had to prepare himself, by hardening the sores which inevitably covered the extremities of knees and elbows; which allowed him, when calloused enough, to climb, but ultimately caused 'sweep's cancer'. The child was deformed in all joints, and in the spine. The best income derived from extinguishing fires (a practice forbidden in the 1788 Act) and boys climbed, in succession, to attack the fire in the flue itself: 'We pin the Bosom of the Shirt, secure it everyway, so that the Fire cannot get at him . . . if he keeps in Motion, the Fire will not lodge; if he is sluggish, he will be likely to be burnt'.

Yet reform did not come easily. The eighteenth-century efforts of Hanway and Porter were followed up by the Radical Member of Parliament, Henry Grey Bennet, who spoke in Byronic tones of 'sacrificing the children of the poor in order to preserve the chimneys of the rich'. But he failed to move the House of Lords, which wrecked Bills in 1817, 1818 and 1819, and the employment of climbing boys was not ended until later in the century.

Apprenticeship, from the first a variable condition, had taken several different courses in response to changing economic circumstances, and in keeping with this, the period ended ambiguously. Children were no longer transported to distant masters to serve seemingly endless indentures, but the abolition of the compulsory seven year clause of the Statute of Artificers did not apply to the pauper children. The workhouse, when the children were not boarded out, substituted for the prentice house for hundreds of children. Was it an improvement? Sir Thomas Bernard's stricture of 1805 would have argued not—'when they [workhouses] become receptacles of youth, they destroy the hope of the succeeding generation'. Parish apprenticeship lingered on until 1844. But its abuse made it no longer correspond to 'the most universally approved part of the Poor Laws'.

WORKHOUSES

The workhouse cast its ominous shadow beyond the Second World War, and its threat is recalled even now by the old. The workhouse had its beginnings in the controversy about the apparently idle in the last decades of the seventeenth century, and the countervailing arguments gave rise to several experiments, of which Cary's in

Bristol was the first to have lasting effect. The Privy Council no longer pressed parishes to setting the poor on work, and the idle hands seemed to many political arithmeticians to constitute a potential source of wealth, given mercantilist organisation. The Utilitarians developed rationalism to a defeatist conclusion, distrusting philanthropy on logical premises. As Pope had put it: 'True SELF LOVE and SOCIAL are the same'.

The eighteenth-century workhouse movement had no comprehensive purpose, nor existence. The poor were in reality not idle by ambition, but by circumstance: few contemporaries understood the function of the economic sponge, which absorbed and rejected labour. And if one attached significance to the visible effects of unemployment, the workhouse offered tempting possibilities. The deserving poor would continue to receive the bounties demanded by law, and the undeserving and industrious would work in a disciplined environment akin to that which the factory was to provide. The workhouse anticipated the factory in many respects, and was largely superseded by it.

Workhouses were no novelty. Apart from such establishments as Bridewell, 'to chastise the vagabond', and the village poor house which sheltered the impotent and aged poor, one was opened at St Giles-in-the-Fields as early as 1641. Experiments recurred at Bristol, Worcester, Plymouth, and Norwich, receiving parliamentary proof in Sir Edward Knatchbull's Act of 1723, which came about two decades after Mackworth's unfortunate Bill. Over one hundred workhouses were soon constructed under the permissive legislation, and were able to make convincing claims, at least with regard to the predominant consideration of economy [**doc. 9**].

The sensible conditions of Gilbert's Act were not obligatory, and the rise of factories and the universality of pauperism in the 1790s led to the abandonment of the workhouse test in 1796. From that point until 1834, outdoor relief under the allowance system matured from a benevolence into a scandal. The workhouses remained full in these infelicitous decades, but their contribution was proportionally diminished.

The parish workhouse was generally dreaded by the poor, if only for its association with uncomfortable death. But it was a refuge from the worst calamities: 'An undoubted claim on such a place was an object of supreme importance to the labourer' (**67**). Diet and comfort, though always Spartan, probably exceeded what the pauper might obtain outside, and while large numbers of poor houses were ramshackle, insanitary and undisciplined, some others were well endowed, with infirmaries and a high degree of regulation.

The organised parish is well demonstrated by St Margaret's, Westminster (**69**). From the initial rental investment in the 'Golden Lion' in 1736, a workhouse grew to cater for 1,000 by 1774, and was supplemented by a new infirmary in 1792 with beds for 300. Even this sizeable effort was insufficient for the 63,982 who comprised the parish register in 1801, and out-relief was enforced in 1797. In keeping, perhaps, with the keen administration, discipline was taut and punishments severe—solitary confinement, bread and water, whipping, and a log of wood affixed to the leg. The men's and women's sides were separated, and husband and wife were parted immediately on admittance. This was by no means universal practice, and Liverpool workhouse even housed married couples apart from the main building. The unpaid directors and guardians visited the parish lunatics regularly, and uncovered on one occasion, in a private asylum at Bethnal Green, inmates chained to the walls and 'wet' patients forced to sleep naked in their spare cots. Yet the energetic responses to this large and growing body of poor are to be commended, though the first Master, a drunken ex-schoolmaster whose standing could not survive the discovery of one of his sons in bed with Mary Salisbury, a female inmate, was a particularly unfortunate selection.

No parish found it easy to find a suitable Master [**doc. 11**], for the workhouse was likely to contain, as did that at Epsom cited by Sir F. M. Eden, 'a driveller', one 'afflicted with leprosy', another 'worn out and paralytic' (**92**). There were also children to deal with, and prostitutes mixed with young children in many crowded wards. Every workhouse therefore adopted its own methods for dealing with offenders. At Wednesbury, for example, the small strong room intended for punishment was rarely used, the governor preferring to chain malefactors and lunatics to the fire grates (**12**).

In no cases were the hopes of profitable industry fulfilled, though they ran sufficiently high for some years to attract joint stock philanthropy. The Liverpool workhouse owed its existence to the capital raised by the trustees of the Charity School, and Alderman Blundell initiated the first project by building thirty-six houses on the south side of the Charity School. The Liverpool institution points to the visionary nature of such hopes, for only twenty of a total of 1,500 inmates were able-bodied, and one-third were under fifteen years of age. It was this factor which was to upset so many assumptions about the poor after 1834. In most workhouses, there were few regular attempts at competitive production, and casual labour was in any case better suited to the broken reeds who teemed there. Typical was the Vestry minute of Wimbledon for 20 May 1753: 'Jo Wilson allowed eighteen pence per dozen for making up into mops all the yarn that is spun in the workhouse, for the use of the parish'.

Disappointment often resulted in torpid administrators farming the poor to a contractor, who was obliged, if he were to manage a business proposition, to skimp amenities [**doc. 10**]. Even in the best-managed workhouses, 'incentives to oppression' existed. The St Marylebone Workhouse had a 'taskmaster', whose remuneration depended on the 2*s* in the £ he was allowed from the proceeds of pauper industry. The human cost of such profits may be imagined (**69**).

However extensive, the workhouse could not accommodate the swelling numbers it was required to house. In Liverpool, where close on 1,500 paupers were receiving indoor relief, an additional 8,000 were in the streets, most of them desperately poor Irish, caught by the tide of the trade failure consequent on the Orders in Council of 1807. Liverpool's situation was particular, and dealt with by an admirably vigilant oligarchy. But the whole policy of indoor relief broke down in the 1790s, and the abolition of the workhouse test only confirmed established practice. The workhouses remained full of the sick and the dying, but outdoor pauperism was infinitely more extensive than indoor, in the final decades of the Old Poor Law.

VAGRANCY

Vagrants comprised a large section of the English poor. Outside the Poor Law—their condition was regulated by the Vagrancy Acts— they numbered 30,000 in Gregory King's estimate 'for the year 1688' (**101**) [**doc. 18**], and were recorded as 60,000 in the parliamentary Select Committee's report of 1821. With his mobility, the vagrant was a source of concern to successive governments, and Parliament frequently reiterated its desire to settle the itinerant poor. That it failed to do so was in no wise due to permissive statutes. Public whipping and then 'removal' to his or her birthplace or last residence' was the vagrant's unhappy lot. The 1597 Act enabled authorities to apply such severity to anyone 'unable to give a good account of himself', which slovenly wording could include all those living an irregular life: the Plymouth Guardians obtained power in 1759 to ship vagrants on board any vessel that would take them. Punishment took no account of the classes of people who might be apprehended, and the sick, lame, and aged were all to suffer the bloody back. They were further assailed by an odious system of rewards which brought the parish officers 5s for each 'idle and disorderly person' arrested within his own parish, and 10s for each 'wandering rogue and vagabond'.

But the authorities went too far in their demands, and the vengeful ferocity of the law drew sympathy for the destitute beggar or sick person. The added supposition that the constable was merely in search of pecuniary reward turned natural sympathy into aggressive support, and the duty of arrest became dangerous in towns. Thus the law's incentives worked counter to its intentions, and sensitised opinion came to object to public whipping. As John Scott expressed it in a pamphlet of 1773, 'who could devote an unhappy human being to the Whipping Post or House of Correction merely for asking for charity?'

The second statutory requirement, that of removal, remained in vigorous operation. Any 'foreign beggars' found in the parish were warned off by its officers, and the justices made use of the 'privy search' to clear a district. But where would those apprehended go? The Bristol Corporation of the Poor complained in 1789 that they all arrived there! In fact, the system added additional numbers to those already on the road, being 'passed' from one parish to the next. Those paupers removed under the settlement laws were conducted all the way by the overseer, whose parish had to foot the bill; but if the poor stranger were a vagrant, the officers had only to hand him over to the neighbouring authority, and the county treasury not only paid the expenses, but actually provided a reward. The vagrant himself gained by an allowance of 6d a day for food, and hence common interest helped litter the roads with the destitute, endlessly travelling.

Parliamentary attempts to prevent the traffic were ineffective, and costs rose so that vagrants were farmed to contractors, who undertook to convey them to their destinations. The transit houses contained many of the abuses associated with workhouse farming:

they were described as filthy and undisciplined, with people thrown together indiscriminately. The Pass House at Liverpool, from which Irish vagrants were reshipped, was particularly squalid.

So many were circulating, on the pass system, that the vagrancy laws were codified in 1824. The Select Committee had euphemistically reported that their shambling progress amounted to 'a pleasurable jaunt' and the resultant legislation was expectedly harsh. The vagrant was henceforth to be treated as an ordinary criminal, imprisoned with hard labour, to apply to the parish officer to be dealt with under the Poor Law if destitute, and to be 'removed' under settlement legislation if applicable. Unhappily for the authorities, the Irish, Scots and Channel Islanders had no place of settlement, since they had no poor law, and the Act was nullified by the increasing numbers of vagrants who claimed an address in Glasgow, or Dublin, or St Hélier, in order to keep on the road. Such paupers were granted licences to beg, and over 3,000 converged on Buckinghamshire each year, calling on local rates for their subsistence.

The vagrant was uncharacteristic of the pauper population, friendless and unwelcome because he was a moving target, yet one which was disturbingly visible. The 'strange beggars, cripples, lusty idle men and women, vagabonds, blind people, pretended and real mad folks, and such like' tramped the highways—the Reverend William Gurney came upon 'not less than 200, with their wives and children' on a journey from Birmingham to London in 1813—and congested at nodal points such as Liverpool and Bath. As with the Poor Law, movement weakened inefficient administration intolerably. The unsettled destitute were always being moved on, expensively but to no destination.

8 Philanthropy

EDUCATION

Practical philanthropy was the outward expression of the Puritan conscience. It was also a justification of the rationale of the individualist morality, whose admiration of the attainment of riches nevertheless 'owed poverty a kind of reverence'. Following the Restoration, the new school of economists advocated a whole new body of social theory: severity towards the weak became regarded as a Protestant duty, as natural compassion was frozen. Suffering could best be relieved by self-help, and the charity school movement matched this mood appropriately.

The moral delinquency of London and the towns, where the children 'swarmed like beasts in the streets', overwhelming the Poor Law officials, prompted the remedy of catechetical instruction for the infant poor. The clergy played a leading part in the provision and management of schools for the poor. But this was not an era of Central Church Funds, or wealthy individual foundations, and the organisation of charity schools, only loosely controlled by the Society for Promoting Christian Knowledge, owed their maintenance to the democratic cooperation of the middle classes: the schools were local enough to stimulate pride of ownership. The Grey Coat Hospital, for example, was founded at St Margaret's, Westminster through the collaboration of six local worthies, including a cheesemonger, a draper, a bookseller, and general dealers in soap, candles, brooms and leather—such persons as 'counted for nothing in the vestry'.

The puritanical middle classes attacked illiterate heathenism with an arid and meagre curriculum. But the aim was limited. The multiplying poor threatened the social structure: discipline through education would diminish that threat. Submission and gratitude were therefore inculcated among the prospective hewers of wood and drawers of water [**doc. 34**].

The instructions prescribed in *The Christian Schoolmaster*, the manual supplied by the S.P.C.K., bear this out. Reading was important mainly as a means to learning the catechism, the Prayer Book, and the Bible. Writing was next favoured, and arithmetic only for the specially able. Girls were included in the scheme of charity education, but instruction inclined naturally towards preparation for domestic service. Some curricula did, however, rise to meet special needs, so that exceptional boys from London charity schools were sent to Neale's Mathematical School to receive vocational training in the art of navigation.

The sober uniform of the charity school—the origin of the Blue, Green, Grey and Yellow Coat Schools—further drove home the lessons of humility and submission. Such distinctive clothing paraded the achievement of the charitable, and did much for public relations. The whole concept, indeed, was dramatised by special charity services which the children attended, marching two by two into church, uniformed and scrubbed, combining military order with the appeal of childhood. And the benefactors in the congregation were silent witnesses to goodness as an accomplished preacher—specially hired for the occasion—delivered his address [**doc. 32**]. The scale of these occasions was vast: a service at St Paul's would attract over 7,000 to join 4,500 children in the ceremony. It is not surprising that such a foregathering should assemble for state celebrations, such as the signing of the Peace of Utrecht, or the recovery of George III. Applause was practically universal, and the Tsar Alexander, author of the Holy Alliance, was moved to tears by the children's rendering of the One Hundredth Psalm.

Such external pomp and circumstance are a reminder that the schools, like all other charities, had to sell themselves. The town was altogether more responsive to the movement than the country, and London enjoyed important advantages. Teachers, clergymen, and bourgeoisie were in better supply, and the London labour market absorbed the products. For similar reasons, urban schools such as those at Bristol and Newcastle-on-Tyne were conspicuous; but country districts faced the insuperable obstacles of agrarian hostility and lack of middle-class leadership. Occasionally, as at Westbury-on-Severn, gentry support would keep a school solvent, and the Governors of the Grammar School opened the Green Coat School at Wakefield in connection with Poor Law administration. Of course, competition from industrialism was severe: dependence on the earnings of child-labour took its toll of attendance, in mining and industrial towns.

Wales, on the other hand, succoured the movement into extraordinary growth. In 1700 there was virtually no Bible-reading or hymn-singing in the land of the bethel. Such evils of omission were assailed by itinerant schools, whose low costs were borne partly by the poor themselves, and partly by the wealthy. Absence of the English emphasis on the drill of attitudes of humility was another individual aspect of the Welsh offshoot. Despite the burial in Chancery of Bridget Bevan's £10,000 trust (for thirty-one years from 1779) the impact was decisive. The Welsh developed a craving for the religious, while maintaining a strong sense of family obligation which enabled the misfortune of poverty to be shared. Religious education was vigorously pursued in Wales, but more than in England for its own sake than as an instrument of oppression.

The effects of offering education to the poor are hard to evaluate but the extent of the effort was such that by 1729 1,419 schools operated in England, with 22,503 enrolled pupils; in the years 1737-1761 3,500 schools in Wales taught some 150,000. The political struggles, absent in Wales, within the movement pushed the Society for Promoting Christian Knowledge into other, missionary, work but numerous schools survived. Endowed schools fared better than subscription, though the Brougham Inquiries of 1818 showed the need for complete overhaul of the administration of charities and the schools, finding diminishing support after mid-century lingered on until they were incorporated with the National School of the nineteenth century.

Commercial patrons, logically, revived demands for schools of industry, first started by Thomas Firmin in 1675, and working schools followed in the wake of workhouses after 1750. If the poor owed their position to idleness, as Defoe had maintained, then they should be set to work. But the organisational strain of showing a profit was too great for the catechetical schools, and the untimely destruction of domestic industry abetted the failure of such institutions.

A more successful development of pauper education was the Sunday School. Robert Raikes opened his first school in Sooty Alley, the chimney sweeps' quarter of Gloucester, in 1780. His aim was to remove the ignorance which caused criminal activity, and a judicious mixture of bribe and punishment pulled in the children, and many adults, on their one free day. Diffusion was helped by the Society for the Establishment and Support of Sunday Schools Throughout the Kingdom of Great Britain (1785), and the Sunday School Union (1803), and opposition was slight in volume and content. The Bishop of Rochester feared the onrush of French Revolutionary ideas, and some Dissenters accused Raikes of Sabbath-breaking; but such sombre orthodoxy was muffled by latitudinarian approval [**doc. 33**]. Queen Charlotte, visiting Mrs Trimmer's Sunday School, 'expressed the most benevolent sentiments and tenderest regard for the happiness of the poor'. Its reformatory powers were most strikingly seen in civilising the miners of the Forest of Dean, 'a most savage race'. The desire of the poor for instruction was clearly strong, and the Sunday School movement went some way towards satisfying it; the Sunday School Society itself reported, after its first quarter-century, the establishment of 3,350 schools educating 275,000 scholars; and this was a fraction of the aggregate.

Brougham's Committee on the Education of the Lower Orders of 1816 drew forth the first composite picture of the poor. While children were attending 18,400 schools, 3,500 parishes 'had not the vestige of a school' [**doc. 20**]. Renewed propaganda in the 1820s produced earnest debates in the reforming Whig Parliament, and, at last, a measure. Althorp's suggestion of £20,000 for education of 'the Children of the Poorer Classes of Great Britain' was carried by 50 votes to 26 on 17 August 1833.

This was the first instance of state intervention in education, and pointed to the failure of organised philanthropy to meet the educational needs of the poor. Schools were inadequate in numbers, and the management of funds had been shown to be corrupt. Instruction was limited and class discipline was imposed by religious sanctions. Yet its achievement was noteworthy. As the historian of the charity school movement puts it, 'the restricted character of Charity School instruction cannot be denied, yet narrow as it was, it was too wide for public taste' (**26**).

HOSPITALS

Trade and commerce bore the overwhelming burden of hospital construction, which magnetised philanthropic funds: the London Hospital averaged £4,300 annually in donations, from 1742 to 1753 (**37**).

The medieval hospital had been concerned with the sick poor rather than the generality of sick persons, and was a charitable refuge for the poor as well as a place for the treatment of disease. Thus, the term 'hospital' was interchangeable with 'almshouse', or 'Maison Dieu'. The growth and accompanying squalor of towns in the seventeenth century rendered such institutions wholly inadequate in intention as in number: plague-infested London supported only two Royal Hospitals, St Bartholomew's and St Thomas's. Out of this need, a more familiar concept of a hospital began to emerge, owing largely to the physicians and surgeons whose laboratory the hospital became. Five of these new hospitals were established in London between 1719 and 1746; only one (Guy's) was the gift of an individual. Thomas Guy was the greatest eighteenth century benefactor, and used the vast fortune accumulated from selling Dutch-printed copies of the English Bible (incidentally infringing the monopoly interests of the King's Printer) to endow 'Mr Guy's Hospital' with £220,000.

But Guy was the exception to the rule of associated philanthropy, which produced, before 1750, hospitals in Edinburgh, Cambridge, Winchester, Bristol, York, Exeter, Northampton, Salop, Liverpool and Worcester. The poor were called on, in these middle-class foundations, to pay fees, for porters, burial deposits, and the like. St Bartholomew's, for example, required 19s 6d on admission—a far cry from the medieval condition of entry, that one must be both sick and poor. Nevertheless, money was vital to the existence of hospitals, and as the schools had popularised their cause, so did the hospitals. The Governors of the Middlesex persuaded David Garrick to give two benefit performances of *Much Ado about Nothing*, and Thomas Arne the composer of *Rule Britannia* offered an Oratorio. Hospital concerts were held in Westminster Abbey.

Naturally, only a fraction of the sick London poor were treated in the hospitals of the metropolis, and a practical additional measure for their care was the Lying-in Charity of 1757, which sent midwives to assist in delivering poor women at home. In its first half-century of operation, the Charity aided 180,000 women—a small link, perhaps, in the vicious circle of poverty and population growth.

The treatment of lunatics underwent some slight change during the eighteenth century. Bethlem, a failure in almost every respect, stopped the admission of sightseers in 1770, and thus deprived itself of the £400 a year which the spectacle had yielded (**37**). St Luke's

Hospital for Lunatics was established in 1751, and was exceptionally well supported. Lack of knowledge, rather than money, held back the treatment of the mentally sick, and the prejudices which herded the feeble-minded together with the indigent in the workhouse, stood in the way of solving other problems implicit in urban over-crowding.

Prostitution and illegitimacy were two such. But the Lock Hospital, founded in 1746, for the relief and rehabilitation of venereal-diseased patients, had to camouflage seamier aspects against narrow-minded sniping. Publicly, it aimed to sponsor 'many innocent women of irreproachable character . . . [who] . . . themselves have received infection from the profligacy of their husbands' (37).

But the representative charity of the eighteenth century was associated with foundlings. There was little evangelical concern for the souls of the children in the aims of Captain Coram, whose compassion for children—he was himself childless—was outraged by the spectacle of abandoned babies. He eventually quarrelled with his fellow governors, but not before interesting the world of 'Quality and Distinction', whose communal patronage of the Foundling Hospital enabled a much lower mortality rate than was common among workhouse children. The bills of mortality for Poor Law children under two years, between the years 1728 and 1750, revealed a casualty rate of 59 per cent, while that of the Hospital, from 1741 to 1756, was 37 per cent. Mothers stormed the doors in the riotous first few days, and the fortunate hundred foundlings admitted was a small proportion of the 'thousands who are still drooping and dying in the hands of the parish nurses'. The size of the problem appeared to grow as it was approached, and the changing perspective was alarming enough to initiate an unusual appeal to Parliament, which responded with an offer of £10,000 in 1756. But it laid down two ruinous conditions. A series of branches was to be established, and the Foundling Hospital had to accept all applicants below a given age, at first two months. On the first day, 117 children were put in the basket hung on the Hospital gates, and in the forty-six months of unrestricted admission 15,000 babies entered the Hospital; 68·3 per cent died. The human tragedy which stares through such bare statistics is distressing, but no more than the realisation that the Foundling Hospital's very survival demanded that the numbers admitted be curtailed. The rare assistance of Parliament, and the interested support of dukes, earls, Sir Robert and Horace

Walpole, Henry Pelham, Hogarth and Handel, failed to prevent the deaths of the thousands of city children, condemned by environment not to taste even the dregs of the Augustan Age.

The mothers of these pathetic babies attracted their share of philanthropy, it is agreeable to record. To avoid their returning to former ways, Robert Dingley got together a committee to found the Magdalen Hospital. Of the original fifty applicants, a number were curiously rejected because they were diseased, and 'one for lack of professional qualifications, being no prostitute'. In the forty-nine years to 1807, the Hospital took in 3,865 penitents, equipping them for better lives with a mixture of useful trades and moral instruction. Critics predictably argued that such humanity would encourage vice. But the Hospital received good financial support, despite the scandal of its first Chaplain, Reverend William Dodd, whose emotional sermons attracted fashionable crowds to Sunday services for the fallen. He was executed for forgery of Lord Chesterfield's signature to a bond. Many of the women's cases were indeed pitiable, without embellishment, and drew forth tearful offerings.

The human wastage of the parish workhouse, together with patriotic feeling, drove Jonas Hanway, like Dingley a merchant in the Russian trade, to action on behalf of destitute and deserted boys. His Marine Society, from its foundation in 1756 until 1815, equipped 31,000 boys for service at sea, enabling them to 'earn an honest livelihood', removed from the temptation of crime arising from dire poverty.

Other, smaller, charities, betokened the remarkable comprehensiveness of the eighteenth-century conscience. A few examples must suffice. Dispensaries, growing in the 1770s and 1780s on the model of the General Dispensary in Aldersgate claimed to treat 50,000 poor annually in the Metropolis, one third of them in their own homes. An assault was made on typhus by the provincial Dr John Haygarth, of Chester, and his methods of treatment by isolation had some success. Even hernia, with its faint appeal, stimulated the charitable impulse: Dr Dorothy George estimated that 10 per cent o: the working population were afflicted (**14**). Businessmen clubbed together in 1786 to finance the National Truss Society. Ten years later followed the Rupture Society, and in 1807, the year of the Ministry of All the Talents, the City of London Truss Society began its active life.

PRISONS AND CRIME

Criminal propensity was not confined to the poor, but there was connective tissue linking pauperism, crime, and overcrowded insanitary gaols.

Accurate statistics are unavailable before the nineteenth century, but the criminal tendencies of the period were repeatedly subjected to pamphleteering scrutiny. The criminal law grew more chaotic as crimes against property increased, and enclosure extended the range of the Game Laws while rising prices pressed men into criminal activity. Yet detection was infrequent by the beadle, constable, and 'night watchmen with rattles', and those who administered the law tempered its vindictiveness with understandable mercy, so that many a delinquent escaped punishment altogether: of 1,601 sentenced to death in 1831, only fifty-two were executed. The more shocking punishments disappeared with the organisation of a police force; branding in 1829, gibbetting in 1834, and the pillory in 1837. How far poverty contributed to crime is an open question, though the interrelation between gin-drinking and criminality would seem to have been firm.

The organisation of gaols was based on a fiscal regimen, from which the poor suffered most. All prisons were royal in theory, but Crown supervision was almost non-existent, and prisons were run by local authorities, private persons, or were farmed out to wardens, whose remarkable intention was to make a profit from their charges. This they effected by the extortion of fees, which were payable for every service, from beds to fresh water. Irons had to be paid for, and Howard found prisoners at Ely Prison, owned by the Bishop, on their backs, chained to the floor by heavy irons (99). Halifax Prison was owned by the Duke of Leeds, and Lord Derby got £13 a year from Macclesfield Prison. No special buildings were employed, and the gaols were overcrowded, unseparated as to sex, and with insanitary conditions which made typhus—'gaol-fever'—endemic.

The houses of correction were intended as 'an adjunct to the relief of destitution', aiming to eliminate the idle, the vagrant, and the unemployed from outdoor relief, later the task of the workhouses. As such, they were under the direct supervision of the justices, who appointed and maintained a master, or governor, and necessary staff. Gradually, though, the penal implication came to dominate the hope of correction by laborious discipline, and in the eighteenth century, the houses of correction 'became instruments more of penal than of Poor Law'. Marking this, an Act of 1720 authorised magistrates to send vagrants to the house of correction or to the common gaol, 'as they thought fit', though the legal distinction was not finally abolished until 1865.

To the modern mind, conditioned to regard personal debt as vital to the economic fabric of the community, imprisonment for small debts may seem the greatest injustice attached to eighteenth century punishment. Trivial sums owed would land a man in gaol, and, once there, fees often exceeded the original debt, and could make his sojourn semi-permanent. General Oglethorpe first revealed the notorious Fleet and Marshalsea Prisons in his Committee of Inquiry of 1729. Prosecutions against Bambridge, Huggins, Acton and Barnes, eventually miscarried, but further Inquiries were inspired by William Hay in 1735 and Oglethorpe, again, in 1754. Their revelations forced an Act of Parliament to make creditors liable to pay a groat (4d) a day for maintenance of their debtors in prison. It was largely a failure, though, as was Oglethorpe's imaginative venture to use debtor prisoners to populate the newly founded colony of Georgia. There was no simple solution for dealing with poor or freed debtors, short of greater permissiveness and/or state interference. Individuals, however, continued to work on their behalf, nagging at public opinion: Roman Catholics showed special concern for the victims of usury, and George I's Turkish valet, Mahomet, secured the discharge of nearly 300 prisoners.

A medical man, William Smith, indicated the nature of the task of reform by this description of Middlesex prisons in 1776:

> Vagrants and disorderly women of the very lowest and most wretched class of human beings, almost naked, with only a few filthy rags almost alive with vermin, their bodies rotting with distemper, and covered with itch, scorbutic and venereal ulcers; ... thirty, and sometimes near forty of these unhappy wretches are crowded or crammed together in one ward.

Torture for extortion; encouragement of drunkenness by the provision of the prison tap; uncontrolled exploitation of women prisoners; the universal prevalence of the custom of 'garnish', whereby every newcomer had to pay a stated sum to provide the whole community with drink, on pain of running the gauntlet: these were more deplorable abuses than bad food and insanitary and damp accommodation, but hardly less prevalent. Such conditions were approached by reformers with the encouragement of Utilitarian/ Evangelical movements, and the continental Enlightenment. Howard startled the reading public [**doc. 35**], but his work had little effect until after his death. The period of attempted reform which ended with the French Revolutionary scare saw a number of useful statutes, and some local progressives such as Sir George Paul in Gloucestershire, the Reverend T. Becher in Nottingham, and Sir T. Beevor in Wymondham, enforced them. But few justices were prepared to adapt, the municipal corporations did nothing, and, ironically, the period of Howard's activity contained the evil of the Thames hulks.

The American War of Independence stemmed the outlet for transported convict labour and prisoners were instead removed to hulks moored in the Thames Estuary and at Portsmouth. Described as 'the most inhumane penitentiaries in existence', they were verminous, overcrowded, and offered a diet of unsaleable ship's biscuit. Transportation was resumed in 1787, to New South Wales, and this applied the principle of punitive hard labour to the poor creatures so sentenced.

A revival of interest in reform occurred about 1810, and Bentham's 1794 proposal for a national penitentiary was readopted through the activity of a group of Members of Parliament, led by Romilly and Burdett. Building actually started in 1811 on the site purchased at Millbank, and though not all of Bentham's provisions for 'the Panopticon' were incorporated, the completed building cost in excess of £500,000, 'the most expensive building since the Pyramids'. Millbank had accommodation for 1,000 men and women. Despite the outlay, the measure fell short of the requirement, which galloped ahead of reform as population density increased the numbers of criminals.

Two women, Elizabeth Fry and Sarah Martin, fired by religious feeling, did important work in the interests of women prisoners. Elizabeth Fry's leading role is common knowledge, and was widely effective, but that of Sarah Martin, herself a poor woman, merits passing reference. This remarkable woman devoted her life to the prisoners of Yarmouth Gaol, gave instruction in sewing, making straw hats, carving spoons from meat bones, and in addition taught prisoners to read and write; she also emphasised after-prison care. Her career, which overlaps the period of this book, is a footnote to the history of British social work.

But of far greater real importance was the work of an administrator. Robert Peel was anything but a sentimentalist, but the beginning he made in central supervision was the greatest contribution to the care of prisoners in the whole period. Peel had no official staff, and his Gaol Act of 1823 relied on the magistracy to submit quarterly reports 'upon every department of prison administration'. Most of the ideas of Howard, excepting the separate cell system, were incorporated. The Act was unevenly adopted, and applied only to prisons under county justices, plus those in London, Westminster, and seventeen other cities and towns. Many of the worst prisons, those in small towns, escaped untouched.

Increasing interest in prisons stimulated public debate, at the end of this period, about whether a prison should punish or reform character. The argument continues today, and then, as now, confused the aims of the reformers. This confusion was reflected in the employment of the treadwheel, which tortured men by the isolation of silence, often intensified by being alongside their fellows on the wheel, while they upheld the Benthamite notion of useful employment. But such an assault on human dignity was an affront to the humanitarians, and the confrontation of the ideas of Association and Isolation was a bitter one. Because of this, uniformity of administration and increased activity by the central government, vital though they were, begged certain questions concerning the functions of prisons.

9 Self-help and Protest

'Collective self-consciousness distinguishes the nineteenth-century working-class from the eighteenth-century mob.' The labouring men of the industrial take-off period did not react passively to un-employment, starvation, political and social ostracism, cultural exclusion. Their interests, abandoned by governments to the harsh mercies of laissez-faire, were defended by an increasingly political conjunction. The image of a cap-doffing peasantry is not easy to break down: there is so little hard evidence, though riots and strikes have a lengthy history. Cottagers, weavers, colliers, and the village poor in general, expressed their feelings through the 'traditional riot' against abuses such as enclosure, the corn bounty, tithes, and the Poor Law itself—workhouses in Suffolk villages were attacked ex-tensively in 1765. The new employee, the townsman, also formed militant ranks, but to seek a range of more political objectives. His relative failure needs to be measured in terms of the relative strength of his adversary. The governing classes were themselves an integral part of that society; not Prussian Junkers dragooning captured estates, nor *Intendants* imposing the will of an arbitrary and distant government. The extensive middle classes, merging imperceptibly into the gentry, had the *commerçant's* stake in internal order, and themselves effected the law in localities, which was where it counted. The apparent tolerance of English society indicated supervisory strength, not weakness. But the lower orders were prepared to batter the establishment, though it must have seemed, and was, pneumatic. Absorbing opposition, it has continued to grow larger and more powerful.

It was assumed and stemmed from the Statute of Artificers (1563), that Parliament and the law should regulate the conditions of labour, and this understanding of legality was the basis of settling disputes. Workers, as well as employers, were protected, and therefore com-binations of work-people (women were often to the fore in early disputes) were unallowable under the law, just as employers were not permitted, theoretically, to fix unjust wages. In preindustrial society, the interests of workers and employers were the same, due to the vertical division of economic society, and thus early combination was not industrial in character. The ethos of the guild was more relevant in most occupations than that of universal brotherhood.

The 'guilty men' were less employers than bakers, millers, dealers and exporters of corn. Granaries and corn mills were destroyed by the Cornish tin miners at Falmouth in 1727, and in succeeding dearths in 1740, 1756–57, 1762, 1766–67, 1770–74, 1782, and 1789, the pattern was repeated. After 1793, the effects were intensified by the war. 'Of some 275 disturbances . . . between 1735 and 1800, two in every three . . . were occasioned by a shortage or sudden rise in the price of food.' Concessions were sometimes obtained. The market at Newbury was invaded on 7 August 1766 by 'a great number of poor people', who 'so intimidated bakers that they immediately fell their bread 2*d* in the peck-loaf and promised next week to lower it to 8*d* a gallon'. Immigrant Irish were another cause of riot, for they threatened customary standards, a factor which contributed to the Gordon Riots (**38**).

Inchoate union activity applied first to those industries which incorporated modern techniques. The woolcombers of the south-west, who met to form a Friendly Society as early as 1700, had a privileged position to uphold, and their nomadic habits took their methods all over England. There was no regard for solidarity, though, and indeed weavers and woolcombers found themselves on opposite sides the weavers taking the employers' side, when Irish worsted yarn was imported into Tiverton in 1749. Pitched battles took place between worker and worker, and when many woolcombers left town (as they also did at Norwich in 1752) the detrimental effect on the weavers was considerable. The position of ownership of machinery was similar among the framework knitters, but here the incendiary issue was the employment of unskilled apprentices, who reduced the employment and wages of adult workers.

The London stocking knitters struck in 1710, and broke knitting frames, and there followed riots and strikes in Nottingham and Leicester. Once more in the textile industry, the silkweavers of East London embarked on a decade of industrial action which ended in 1773, with a confirmation of sixteenth-century regulations. A battalion of guards was necessary to take possession of materials, and the workers marched on Westminster when confronted by French imports. The rebellious state became permanent after 1769. The famous Spitalfields Act which concluded the affair, laid down standards of rules and pay, under periodic control by the magistracy. A union was formed (and permitted even after the Combination Acts) to see that the Act was carried out. The weavers, in effect, had regained the protection of a Parliament still committed to a prescriptive role in industrial relations.

Parliament, if unsure of its legal obligations, was certainly unsympathetic to combinations, and prohibited such formations by tailors in 1721 and 1767, in the woollen trade in 1726, in silk, linen, cotton, fustian, iron, and leather in 1749, by hatters in 1777, and papermakers in 1797: 'Parliament from the beginning of the eighteenth century was perpetually enacting statutes forbidding combinations in particular trades' (**43**). These merely supplemented official labour regulations; by 1799, however, the situation was different, enough to revolutionise policy. Intervention had become discredited, the whole apparatus of Tudor supervision outmoded by novel industrial techniques. Economic growth, it was plausibly argued, required freedom for experiment and change, and this condition allowed no authority to the gilds, needed no trained apprentices to mind machines. Such considerations had already begun to determine new policy when Adam Smith's *Wealth of Nations* (**107**) gave ideological support to a 'practice to which experience had repeatedly driven statesmen'. From the labourer's standpoint, on the other hand, the Industrial Revolution developed an exposed position in which protection was never more desperately required. Authority was fumbling in its reaction, as the machine drove employers and their work-folk into increasing dichotomy.

The Combination Acts of 1799 and 1800 were passed as a political measure, to lessen the feared possibility of men combining to effect a Jacobin takeover. The fear may have been justified; the irony was that repression had the effect of associating the Jacobin revolutionary tradition with illegal unionism, creating a clandestine industrial and political organisation which aimed at revolution.

That some forty Acts of Parliament had earlier been passed to prevent workers combining evinced widespread existence of the practice, but the Combination Acts were wholesale in their application, and inaugurated a quarter-century when 'justice was entirely out of the question' according to Francis Place, who manoeuvred their repeal in 1824. The accused was denied trial by jury, and was judged by his accusers, the justices. This partisan measure withdrew the poor man's rights while exposing him to the operation of free labour laws, 'one of the most humanly degrading dogmas in history' (43). Curiously, though, trade unionism made great advances during the prohibition era; a strike was usually necessary before the Acts were invoked, and persecution was unsystematic. Nevertheless, the Combination Acts were no dead letter for the workers, as they were for their employers [**docs. 36, 37**].

What did follow was the most romantic phase of working-class history. Association was driven underground, and secret meetings took place on moors, under hedgerows, but more commonly in sympathetic taverns. In addition, the swearing of oaths, elaborate initiation ceremonies, and hidden or buried union documents, gave a conspiratorial air to the development of an authentic collective spirit.

More important to growth than secrecy was the cover afforded by Friendly Societies. These had early origins, and were organised mainly by skilled artisans who contributed funds to 'the box', to insure against sickness, unemployment, and, ultimately, a pauper burial. A decent send-off has long been valued among the working class, and the tradition persists in numerous 'death and dividend' societies. As artisans joined the destitute in the 1790s, Benefit Clubs extended their shelter to many organisations founded primarily for industrial purposes. Under the shelter of George Rose's Act of 1793, they flourished where other clubs perished, so that by the end of the wars, in 1815, 925,429 members had purchased an individual right to relief, by payment of a weekly subscription of 2d or 3d. The societies paid 6s or 7s a week, which lightened the burden of the parish poor rate, and in few respects was the Poor Law more closely identified with political decisions. Keeping down the Poor Rate was reason enough for their continued encouragement, but had to be balanced against the Jacobin danger of club meetings. In fact, Friendly Societies gave financial assistance during a turnout (in Manchester, strike payment amounted to £1,500 a week), and the Cotton Spinners Association developed union aspirations from the formation of Benefit Clubs in Oldham and Stockport, in 1792. However, their scattered distribution and lack of total class comprehension—the Newcastle Friendly Society allowed 'no Pitman, Collier, Sinker, or Waterman to be admitted'—limited their threat.

Luddism, by contrast, was 'a movement of the people's own', as Cobbett had it. There were three main regions—Nottinghamshire, the West Riding, and Lancashire—supporting three major textile industries—of lace, wool and cotton—facing a crisis of overproduction for markets shrunk by French restrictions. Its causes were more profound than the immediate situation created by the Orders in Council, though, and its character had some breadth. For the Luddites were opposing the termination of paternalist government, and their cause was embraced by public opinion generally in the Midlands and the West Riding, where small owners still prevailed: theirs was no mere bread riot, though the political element may have been 'intrusive rather than intrinsic' (**38**). Laissez-faire advanced rapidly, following the Combination Acts. Wage and price fixing had long been neglected, but they remained legal obligations until the onslaught of the early nineteenth century: woollen trade regulations were suspended between 1803 and 1808, and repealed in 1809; in 1813 apprenticeship clauses of the Statute of Artificers went (for all but parish children); and 1814 saw the termination of the magistrate's duty of enforcing a minimum wage. The labourers were by these means 'thrust beyond the pale of the constitution', and the imposition of a free labour market meant depressed living standards, in the short term. Almost half the Yorkshire shearmen were out of work from 1806 till 1817, and a quarter of the population of Nottinghamshire were on parish pay. The years of Luddite activity looked back to Tudor wage regulation, forward to Trade Unionism. The new working class, having lost the right of association in 1799, now had legal state protection removed: as Sir Walter Scott wrote to Southey, 'You are quite right in apprehending a Jacquerie, the country is mined beneath our feet'.

The most noteworthy feature of the actual disturbances was that of organisation. Working in secrecy, men were drawn together to central points at night, supplied with muskets, hatchets and hammers, and directed to chosen objectives. Clearly the movement was regional, but this is not to deny the existence of co-ordination, and certainly Luddism has a more impressive record in this respect than comparable English movements. The security was remarkable.

Agitation for Parliamentary Reform began, and Hampden Clubs originated, at exactly the point where Luddism ended, destroyed by improved trade conditions and the widespread employment of government agents, along with the 12,000 troops barracked between

71

Leicester and York. From 1815, the lower orders were held down by force, and union activity centred on the need for social and factory reform, rather than the 'moralising of Cobbett' or Huntite Radicalism. The British working class—by now an entity—formed itself into clubs and organisations of all kinds, following the long custom of Dissent: 'half a dozen working men could scarcely sit in a room together without appointing a Chairman, raising a point-of-order, or moving the Previous Question' (43).

The massacre of Peterloo, carried out mainly by the volunteer Yeomanry, was a pitiful episode, and occasioned the formation of scores of clubs, many directed towards revenge. But the emphasis became political during the next decade, and leadership went to the Utilitarians and the younger Whigs. The illegal press of the period of the Gagging Acts was political also, and contributed to a period of optimism regarding constitutional means to reform, the poorer people having, at this stage, no literature of escapism, the Gothic diet served up by Victorian publishers. But such developments reached down only to the level of the artisan, restored to economic vigour by the expansion of trade in the 1820s. Owenism and the unions which followed the repeal of the Combination Acts was rapid, but it was in the rural Speenhamland counties that the last protest, the 'Swing' riots, of 1830, came.

These riots were much closer in character to the starvation riots which have punctuated all recorded history. Apolitical in outlook, they affected tens of thousands, 'exasperated into madness by insufficient food and clothing', and were characteristic of older social organisation in enabling labourers and small farmers to present a united front. The 'last labourers' revolt' followed from multiple causes, summarised by Dr Rudé as 'tithes, rents, wages, pauperism and poverty, agricultural depression, poaching and the game laws, and radical agitation' (38, 72). The introduction of threshing machines and the employment of immigrant Irish labour (22) ignited the mixture: barns and cornstacks were burnt—'fires make a good argument', said Carlyle—and threshing machines were destroyed in an outbreak which swept through the south-east of the country, consuming property in sixteen counties.

The government reacted with a savagery equalled during the Bristol riots of 1831, when the rioters, 'who completely destroyed . . . forty-two Dwelling Houses and Workhouses', were charged by the military. One hundred and twenty were killed or wounded, and 250 sabred. At the trial, five were sentenced to death. Again, this was a disturbance in the traditional pattern, an undisciplined assault on property releasing pent-up frustration. Its interest lay in its limited intention. The poor who burned and looted were living near the bread-line, and they had little prospect of any amelioration from a constitutional direction. Aliens to the political state, they yet had no specific grievance. Against what authority could they seek redress; whose responsibility was their hungered circumstance? The elusiveness of the target determined the wildness of the aim, and while the Luddites had attacked not only machines, but the withdrawal of state protection, both themes were becoming outdated by 1834. The mature working class turned to trade unions, and a class war, leaving as a bitter memory 'bargaining by riot'. Essentially, it was the protest of the fundamentally helpless, worth recording to dispel inadequate notions of a supine peasantry. At least the period ends with martyrs to a cause, for the Tolpuddle oath-takers initiated an heroic and purposeful period of intervention by the Common People.

Solace 10

DRINK

The poor had their compensations: slums bred overcrowding, but also engendered companionship and communal fellowship. Many of the diversions which absorbed the energies of moral reformers were damnable, yet in sweeping them away, the reformers piled up others. Thus hard drinking and chapel-going, though in diametric contention, provided outlets for men driven to escape: they were related to each other, both giving solace to the poor.

Between these extremes, there were other recreations, largely reprehensible to modern sensibility, of crude sports and pastimes. As in all other fields, however, the poor did not speak in their own defence: their subculture was illiterate. When it was described, it was defamed. Bull-fighting has its Hemingway; but bull-baiting remained undefended by any advocate.

The cultural patterns of the poor were disorganised, and much of what we might know of custom has been lost with the dying generation. This is specially the case with folk-song. For early industrial expression was oral, and while the Negro spiritual endures as a moving testimony to the tragic condition of the American slave, no such proximity of feeling can be gained with the economic slave of eighteenth century England.

It would be wrong, however, to sentimentalise the lives of the poor, through ignorance of their true plight. Bestiality stands as a major theme: 'the passing of Gin Lane, Tyburn Fair, orgiastic drunkenness, animal sexuality and mortal combat for prize money in iron-studded clogs, calls for no lament' (43). But the springs of such behaviour must be investigated—'all social organisms secrete their own toxins' (42).

Nothing is more closely identified with the poor of this period than drink, for example. Yet it is well to note that no strong body of opinion advocated temperance during our period. Ale-drinking was an essential feature of the diet of all classes of society, in the absence of other beverages, or even of pure water, and it was extolled as a patriotic virtue. John Bull has a pot of ale in his hand, a barley corn in his hat, and a toper's paunch. Protestantism, constitutional government, and beer were bracketed in the popular mind, in opposition to Catholic autocracy and wine. How much the poorer classes actually consumed is difficult to estimate. Gregory King calculated that the poor spent more on beer than on any other household commodity, and that the average household spent more on beer than on milk, butter and cheese, put together. It was a staple of rural society, at all levels, and abstinence was in any case out of the question due to lack of substitutes. One of the evil consequences of gin-drinking was considered to be that less malt was drunk, and Doctor Johnson could remember the time when 'all the decent people of Lichfield got drunk every night and were not the worse thought of'. Beer was regarded by agricultural workers, miners, and steel-workers as essential for heavy labour, 'to put back the sweat', an indulgence which broke monotony. It was therefore a cultural as well as a dietetic matter, though beer and porter may have helped balance an inadequate diet—a claim which certainly could not be made for gin.

Government favour for this growth industry had its origins in the political Francophobia of William III and the economic condition of a grain-exporting nation. Statutes in William's reign, reinforced under Anne and the Hanoverians, encouraged distilling from home-grown wheat and barley, provided a market for farmers' surplus cereal crops, and, by attacking importation of French brandy, gave to gin and whisky a patriotic flavour. (The political connotation has probably been exaggerated; the great Whig, Sir Robert Walpole, preferred claret to port, 'the squire's drink' (**71**).) The spirit was sold in the most demoralising circumstances, and was cheapened by compound distillers, who added aniseed, juniper berries, etc., to the malt spirit, and redistilled the liquor after 'lowering' it with water. The practice, which produced a fiery potation, was illegal, but difficult to suppress.

Gin was sold in the most demoralising circumstances. The scene has been immortally depicted by Hogarth, the decrepit horrors of whose Gin Lane are meant to be contrasted with the affluence of Beer Street. It is hard to argue that he took artistic licence. In 1726, every fifth house was reported to be a 'dram shop' in some parishes, and it was observed that spirit was retailed from wheelbarrows in the street, or 'privately in garrets, cellars, back-rooms and other places'. A committee appointed to investigate sanitary precautions noted the 'violent fondness and desire of this liquor, which unaccountably possesses all our poor'. At Holborn workhouse, 'Geneva is clandestinely brought in among the poor there, and they will suffer any punishment . . . rather than live without it' (**14**). Gin houses were also brothels and places for receiving stolen goods, and although the signboard 'Drunk for 1*d*, dead drunk for 2*d* with clean straw for 1½*d*' is put down to sardonic cockney humour, it seems difficult to overstate the horrors of the great gin-drinking period, 1720–50.

Contemporaries condemned the evil, and opposition succeeded in breaking down the vested interests which employed emotive arguments about 'the liberty of the people'. Petitions came in from doctors, magistrates, and industrial towns, and the press joined the campaign, relating drink, crime and poverty in an early example of the force of extra-parliamentary public opinion: more, its success showed the extreme concern at the threat of cheap liquor, and it is little short of remarkable that spirit consumption should have been checked at a time when corn prices were still low. Things improved after 1751, but strong spirit remained a killer; only it became more expensive. The police magistrate, Colquhoun, made the following interesting observation during the prohibition of distilling in 1795: 'The poor were apparently more comfortable, paid their rents more regularly and were better fed than any period for some years before . . . this can only be accounted for by their being denied the indulgence of gin, which became in great measure inaccessible from its very high price.' Gin-drinking may be assumed to explain why times of cheap corn did not bring relief from poverty [**doc. 22**]. It was a disease of poverty, 'a passion among beggars and inmates of workhouses and prisons', and poverty caused the craving for the warmth and oblivion so economically acquired: tragically, poverty was also the result.

SPORTS AND PASTIMES

Other pastimes of the poor were, if not invariably drunken, then circumscribed by ignorance and want of public holidays. Most were brutal, and provided the maximum of boisterous escapism permitted by the law (bears and bulls, for example, were not allowed to be killed by their tormentors). Inflicted pain gave pleasure to all classes, and human suffering had a special attraction: the humane Parson Woodforde gave his servants time off to see a hanging in Norwich, and the Tyburn executions caused widespread absenteeism once every six weeks. At the base of society, indifference to suffering was a concomitant of existence, and it was not to be expected that a brutalised people should seek edifying recreation. For those who did seek, they may have found aesthetic consolation in natural surroundings, for England was a beautiful country where the labouring classes lived out their lives, and even advanced urbanisation retained pastoral affiliations. D. H. Lawrence held that it was 'ugliness which betrayed the spirit of man'. But he was writing of the nineteenth century.

Baiting bulls and bears remained legal until 1825 and 1835 respectively, and it was believed that any animal dying immediately after violent exertion, coursed hare, for example, would be the more tender for the experience. The baiting was accordingly carried out by the butcher, who kept special dogs for the purpose. The bull was tethered to a 25-yard-long rope, attached to a stake, and bull-dogs, carefully trained and proudly 'ondled', aimed to pin the bull to the ground.

Shocking atrocities accompanied the affair, as dogs were commonly gored and bulls mutilated to induce ferocity, tortured out of exhaustion by straw fires lit under them. The poor of Bethnal Green had a variation, known as 'bullock-hanking', which outraged the rector: 'I have seen them drive the animal through the most populous parts of the parish, force sticks pointed with iron up the body, put peas into the ears, and infuriate the beast, so as to endanger the lives of all persons passing along the streets'. Bear-baiting was less prevalent in our period, and was dying out after the mid-seventeenth century, presumably from lack of bears.

Of course, bulls had to be killed, and slaughter-house practice of the time was not for the squeamish, but such justification could not be made on behalf of cock-fighting. This was, and remains, a vicious and degrading business; yet it was patronised by all classes, maybe for its wagering potentiality.

Such contests frequently took place at fairs, or wakes, which had a cultural importance for poor people as well as an economic significance. The hardships of the poor were alleviated or diverted, infrequently in post-Reformation England, by 'feast-days', when a 'bit of beef' and gingerbread, fruit, toys and ribbons, could all be bought. These 'tides' were patronised by the lowest classes, and 'pedlars, sharpers, gypsies, ballad-mongers, and hawkers' provided a colourful contrast to everyday tedium. Authority disapproved, usually. At a time of dearth in Bolton (1783) a magistrate reported 'a very large procession of very young men and women with fiddles, garlands, and other ostentations of rural finery . . . merely to celebrate . . . a fair at a paltry thatched alehouse upon the neighbouring common'. As many as six bulls would be subjected to 'canine encounter' at wake time, and drunkenness was always present, as at public celebrations of great events. At royal births the ale was often free.

Spectator sports such as pugilism were the more prevalent, but the lower orders chased rowdily after footballs down village streets: Cricket had not yet reached the industrial districts, and Trevelyan's 'squire, farmer, blacksmith and labourer . . . at ease and happy all the summer afternoon' has a distinctly impressionistic atmosphere (44). It is fair to record that cricket inspired the first recognition of the social value of recreation, when the boys of the Marine Society were organised to play the game in the later eighteenth century.

Lack of legitimate outlet for amusement and exercise led to many of the excesses noted among rioting London apprentices, and the magistracy were concerned to put down all forms of public entertainment, gaming-houses, bull-baiting, cocking, fairs, public-shows; even the gathering of hazelnuts brought prosecution in Sheffield (1812), and Sunday activities were particularly proscribed. The Society for the Suppression of Vice was active and successful. Under the direction of Wilberforce, 623 successful prosecutions for breaking Sabbath laws were brought between 1802 and 1810.

Thus sport, overwhelmingly the preoccupation of the contemporary worker, was infrequent and stifled. The idea of beneficent recreation was imperfectly understood, if at all, and a cultural dimension, rather than extending the labourer's experience, tended further to brutalise his existence, to emphasise its earthiness.

INDUSTRIAL RELIGION

The Anglican Church re-emerged from the Interregnum exclusive and sectarian, tied to the rulers for mutual safety against the levelling tendencies of Puritan concepts. Doctrinally, the eighteenth century concerned itself with rational discussion of unitarianism or deism. The 'cosmic battles' of Milton and Bunyan were perhaps too enervating to be sustained, and the English Church found its role settled in the depths of quiescence: enthusiasm was the great vice (**39**). There was little in eighteenth-century Anglican services to disturb the gentry in their somnolent observance, for the 'pathological dread of fanaticism' ruled out emotional appeals (services were read, not sung, in the early part of the century) and the detached refinement of Anglican worship expressed the cultivated society which embraced it as its own. The poor could scarcely identify with such an institution. There were concerned and humane vicars of the Church, naturally, and its vices of too easily camouflaged solid virtues, but the generality held good, of complacent and lethargic men, whose social status isolated them from the poor.

The failure of the national Church to achieve comprehension spoke for the vigour of dissenting religion in seventeenth-century England; but there was little sympathy with poor folk from this direction. The views of Tawney (**42**) and Weber (**51**) on this subject have earlier been mentioned, but it is worth reiterating that those whose religious disabilities excluded them from the post-Restoration settlement had little in common with those disqualified on economic grounds. Dissent sided with the strenuous, and the Quakers owed no debts to indolence, as they founded business empires. Moreover, Calvinistic doctrines of the elect saw the poor, the 'corrupt lump', as existing outside grace. The lowest orders were excluded religiously, as well as socially and economically. Closest to the poor in social membership among the sects were the Baptists. Bunyan wrote as a poor man, and E. P. Thompson (**43**) sees *Pilgrim's Progress* as one of the 'two foundation texts of the English working-class movement', along with Thomas Paine's *Rights of Man*.

Dissent fell short of universal acceptance among the plebeian ranks mainly because of the widely held notions of the elect, and because its preaching was too intellectual in character. The blinkering nature of Calvinism itself militated against welcoming the growing masses after 1750. Thus the Calvinist Puritan sects were closing their ranks at the very time of potential recruitment. Offering so little to the dispossessed, they allowed the task, curiously, to fall on members of the established Church.

Analysis

Religious succour for the poor was inspired by a Church of England Tory, John Wesley. His political intentions, unlike those of Dissent with its promise of radicalism, were conservative, and so were his religious origins. But Wesley did not sell in orthodox markets: for the first time, he took religious doctrine to the new labouring population of 'uncouth colliers, sweated nailers'. His message reached the unevangelised poor and social outcasts, whose helplessness under the temporal oppression of the mine and furnace caused them to grab at any spiritual straw. What a promise the afterlife held! For Wesley not only asserted the equality of the poor with the rich in the race for Heaven, but held up the picture of torments to come for their oppressors (**111**).

Yet the Methodists did not represent any fundamentally new dogma. Their novelty was organisational. John Wesley personified the view of history as a travel agent; in covering a quarter of a million miles throughout Britain before his death in 1791, he preached wherever a congregation could be gathered. The camp meetings, classes, and circuits, stimulated latent potential which was to contribute decisively to nineteenth-century political movements. The immediate effects were to develop communal outlets for the poor, to give them the opportunity to savour public speaking and administration. This 'school for democrats' militated against Wesley's Toryism, and for the first time exercised the poor's mind, atrophied by cultural barrenness and social isolation.

Even allowing that Methodism took religion to the people, it is nevertheless surprising, at first sight, that they accepted the offering. Methodism reinforced the complaint that the labouring classes were idle, but re-emphasised the traditional Christian tenet of the blessedness of poverty, a teaching which gave to the poor the incentives of those bound by authoritarianism—of long-term rewards. Miserable and depressed in the extreme, the industrial worker's prison appeared inescapable; within its walls indoctrination techniques had some chance of success. Children had put before them the expectations which sober submission to poverty would bring: moral regeneration was to come out of physical degeneration. This pull towards despairing chiliasm was equalised by emotional propaganda. Religion consoled the masses who responded with tears and groans, who swooned and were overtaken by paroxysms. 'For the miner or weaver, the Chapel with its . . . music and singing, took the place that the theatres, picture galleries, operas, occupied in the

80

lives of others' (**18**). The sensual and erotic imagery of its hymns, the violence of its language, laid Methodism open to the charge of depredation. Leigh Hunt wrote in 1809, 'If God must be addressed in the language of earthly affection, why not address him as a parent rather than a lover?' Other Methodists, such as the remarkable Joanna Southcott, developed a cult of the poor: her God announced, 'my judgment must be great in the land, if they starve the poor in the midst of plenty'.

Evangelism dug at several layers of society, but it is undeniable that it converted numbers of 'the lowest and most debauched strata of the labouring poor'. Fulfilling a dual role as the religion of exploiter and exploited, its numerical success should not be exaggerated, especially in the most apathetic rural parishes. 'Vital religion' claimed an approximate 60,000 footholds in 1789, and had erratically reached 237,000 by 1827; the Primitive Methodists, whose 'chapels were the coal-pit banks', and who were themselves of the working class, had only 7,842 followers in 1842. Recruitment, interestingly, reached peaks during periods of political despair, but the connection between political, social, and religious attitudes is as yet only tentative (**46**) and many Methodists, sharing Wesley's own Toryism, hated democracy as much as sin.

For all its emotional excesses and spiritual autocracy, the incursion of Methodism into the lives of the common people was largely beneficial. Its effect was not everywhere felt, nor was it permanent, but Wesley and his followers did do something to uplift the hearts and minds of colliers and tinners, the profligate and the destitute, if only towards the intangible. If nothing else, the acceptance of Methodism helps to demonstrate the abject hopelessness of 'Christ's poor'.

Part Three

ASSESSMENT

Assessment

Poverty preoccupied social and economic thinking throughout the period 1660–1834. Its elemental structure was yet never—even in 1834—defined by officialdom, and the position of the authorities was nightmarishly to see their attempts to improve a present situation successively negated by new and unforeseen factors. Measures adopted as palliatives tended to worsen the situations they sought to cure. The sequence of misgovernment and mischance accompanying the spread of pauperism can stand as the dominating features of the eighteenth century, once the modulated surface of culture and society is penetrated. For the period was a Utopian interlude for the aristocracy, when all that was representative of a patrician style of living flourished in England as never before or since. The contrasting existence of poor folk, of grinding, asymmetrical realism, gives the Poor Law, a specially dramatic appeal, heightened by the tension between leniency and severity, uncontrollable wars and population growth, and the denouement of 1834. Despite this, society achieved cohesion to an extent hardly paralleled elsewhere in Europe, as social responsibility developed alongside privilege.

This condition remained until 1834. Until then, administration was local, expedient and unpredictable: the Poor Laws, unsupported by compulsion or a civil service, never grew into a comprehensive and national system.

Neither the expectation, nor the intention, of the Elizabethan legislators had been to abolish the scourge of poverty. Those realists sought only to deal with occasional periods of distress, and minister only to the unable poor (**28**). Industrial employment was unknown to them, and incapacity from the economic conditions was not envisaged. Hence the 'deserving poor' were a separable category. As increasing population and spreading urban conditions blurred the divisions between the poor, all came to call on this benevolence. The insecurity of existence was finite in some directions, at least. While not extravagant to modern considerations, parish relief was generous enough to bring forth criticism from mercantilists, advocating a low-wage economy and the necessity to enforce dedicated toil: 'everyone but an idiot knows that the lower classes must be kept poor, or they will never be industrious' (Arthur Young). Sickness and old age were provided for with variable effectiveness; and however low the standards may have dropped, sights were consciously lowered in 1834, with the use of relief as a deterrent.

The Poor Law, for the majority, was the only available recourse in times of hardship. Private charity continued to flourish after the Restoration (37) but it was far too arbitrarily dispersed to deal with so huge a demand. Its major success was to keep the pauper population controlled, and may be explained by the negative consideration that no government, despite intense strain, had to contend with a second Peasants' Revolt, or a first social revolution. The rioting which accompanied hard times, bad harvests or bad trade, was intermittent, and does nothing to indicate deep-seated resentment or total despair. It was, indeed, occasionally political in temper, but the masses demonstrated throughout the period a tranquillity and acceptance, and for this the Poor Laws must take some credit. The lower classes had some sense of social protection, and regarded it as a right. It was a claim that the governing class could ill afford to ignore.

It was, however, in this local paternalism that many of the abuses of the Poor Laws had their origin. In most important respects legislation was benevolent in intent, but parochialism is one charge the Poor Laws cannot evade. It was one of the piles of the administrative structure, and, though eroded in time by the flooding of the urban masses, served well enough the conditions for which it was created. Furthermore, ignorance about handling large organisations was a shortcoming of the time. Independently, within small village units, pauperism was manageable; nationally, the size of the problem became frightening in times of distress. For this reason, and because the Poor Laws were so deeply ingrained a part of society, the poor continued to be at the behest of local interests. Reformers procrastinated, because real change would entail revolution: an administrative revolution was exactly what did occur under the Whig government of the 1830s.

Any assumptions about the effects of the system on the poor themselves must remain uncorroborated, and this is an important limitation. Nonetheless, it is possible to stress some of the short-comings. The right of relief could be asserted only in a single parish, a provision intensified by the Act of Settlement. This imposed a severe restriction at a time when economic forces, ranging from enclosure to a declining death rate, acted to drive people away from their places of legal settlement. The migrant put himself at con-siderable risk, and though young and able men did circumvent the law, the ultimate result was often degrading removal. The laws of settlement were also responsible for the inquisition into the private lives of the poor. Putative fathers of bastards were forced to the altar, often on the flimsiest evidence; men were forced to reveal their credentials to secure a settlement and the law was over-employed in the service of diminishing the poor rate [**docs. 25, 26**]. The pauper, in a country practising the philosophy of freedom, was marked out and could be forcibly returned to a workhouse, imprisoned as surely as a political detainee in a police state. Apprentice laws were also perverted, diverting the young into unskilled occupations which were followed in conditions of servitude.

Economic revolution hastened changing attitudes and policy. Freedom for commerce and industry was sound enough economic dogma, but could be inhuman in its application. Rousseau answered his query, 'why is it that in a thriving city the Poor are so miserable?' with the response that it is a natural consequence of freedom that some are reduced to want. The sentiment was ruggedly defined by Dr Johnson, when comparing marriage and celibacy with freedom and servitude, that the one has many pains, the other no pleasures. Where it had been possible to argue for education and houses of industry, as a constructive contribution to the great 'Debate on the Poor' in the earlier period; later pamphlets refuted such ideas, lest labourers should aim beyond their station, and abandoned hopes of the weakest section of the population yielding profit in competition with factory industry. New situations made old solutions untenable. Reliance on workhouses, always optimistic, became absurd in the 1790s, when the designation of the 'labouring poor' attached to so many. A system of embryonic family allowances, Speenhamland, was widely taken up by bemused parish officials. Such a withdrawal to outdoor benefit sharpened discussion, and threw theory and practice into paradoxical relief. For this was the period when Malthus' law of population, reinforced by Ricardo's 'iron law' of wages (**105**) and the efficiency bent of the philosophical radicals, pointed straight at harsh treatment for the lower orders: yet at that very time, poor rates reached their peak, and charity became synonymous with wages. The explanation was that the ruling orders feared revolution more than the costly and demoralising effects of state charity.

Such extensive, and wasteful, benevolence, ensured abolition of the old system as soon as political confidence returned, which it did when the 1830 election was won on a reform platform. The Commission of 1832 provided exhaustive evidence—5,000 pages of it—in support of change. Of course, the politically irrelevant poor did not contribute to the determination of their own destiny, and their fate was committed to the hands of Edwin Chadwick, to the doctrine of 'less eligibility'. Thomas Carlyle's view determined their miserable lot in the years to come: 'if paupers are made miserable, paupers will needs decline in multitude. It is a secret known to all rat-catchers'.

Despite its inconsistency, as individual as the men who organised it, the Old Poor Law was not fatuously inadequate, as the commissioners of 1834 made it appear by selecting facts and special pleading. The connection between Speenhamland and large families was exaggerated by contemporaries, and the application of outdoor relief did at least as much to avert revolution as the application of political repression. 1834 was as reticent as 1601 about the causes of poverty, and this omission caused Speenhamland to be too often misinterpreted in the discussion about the 'principle of 1834'. Econometric study might reveal its true worth, but for the present it is enough to generalise in an opposite direction to the traditional, and assert that social and political stability, long esteemed as a uniquely British achievement, owed a sizeable debt to the relatively liberal distribution of poor relief. And if, as Lord Townshend held, the Poor Law was a 'gigantic subsidy to wages' (**22**), it helped technological progress by reducing manufacturing costs; the system staved off the fate of so many expanding communities, the shortfall of resources.

Any conclusion about the problems associated with poverty in this period is weakened by the heterogeneous nature of the operation of the Poor Laws, by the lack of adequate analysis of returns by the Commissioners of Inquiry, and, most grievously, by the absence of an authentic voice of the poor [**doc. 39**]. Equally, the dangers of judging the ethical values of another age are all too evident: 'Sympathy is never the same thing as experience.' If every age creates its own abuses, then that of the eighteenth century was of an administrative rather than a legislative nature. To qualify from contemporary countries, and contemporary opinion—upper class though it was—the period of 1660–1834 did not substantially fail to live up to Doctor Johnson's absolute dictum, 'a decent provision for the poor is the true test of a civilisation' [**doc. 38**]. Poverty remained a relative problem; it could have become a catastrophe.

Part Four

DOCUMENTS

ettlement was a right worth struggling for, but the poor man was
required to submit himself to scrutiny by the magistrates, a process which
expended unjustifiable amounts of ratepayers' money. If settlement was
unproven, the pauper was removed from the parish. The vagrant, on the
other hand, was dealt with directly under the Vagrancy Acts, straight-
forward but cruel.

document 1

The Examination of Edward Tyner. 1744

This Examt. upon his Oath saith that abt. 18 years ago he hired
imself to live as a Hired servt. by the year to One Benja. Smith
f the parish of Wimbledon yeoman at Six Pounds a year Wages,
aith he Continued with his sd. Master In the sd. parish of
Wimbledon One year and a half under the above Contract &
ecd. his said wages accordingly, Saith that he has lived ever
since in the hamlet of Rowhampton & in the parish of Wands-
worth In the sd. County of Surrey but did not gain any legall
settlemt. In either of the two last mentioned places, either by
aying the Poors Rate, Renting Lands or Tenemts. of the yrly.
value of ten Pounds, Serving an Parochial Office, or by any
other Means Whatsoever. Saith that abt. 16 years ago he Inter
Married with Elizabeth his now Wife by whom he hath had two
children, both now living, namely Elizabeth aged ten years &
upwards & Edward aged three yrs. & upwards.

the Mark of

Not sworn.
X

Edward Tyner

From the *Wimbledon Examinations Book, no. 28.*
Surrey Record Office P5/5/208.

document 2

forcible removal

An examination of a witness for a coroner's inquest on a poor man found
in a field at Ham. He was forcibly removed by officers of the hamlet of
Ham and left to die in Kingston. Had he remained in Ham, he would
have been a charge on the poor rate, which would have provided his
burial expenses.

Joseph Godding of Kingston upon Thames in the County of
Surrey deposes on his oath that on Fryday last the first of this
Instant February about 6 o'clock in ye Evening John Cope of
Ham and Mr Townsend brought a Poore Man (whose name
the deponent is informed was James Bowen) in a Cart and that
they said they put the said James Bowen out of ye Cart into the
Street near ye Stockhouse in Kingston and declared they would
there leave him which they accordingly did, and this Deponent
saies that the same James Bowen was then almost expiring and
Dyed in ye Street soon afterwards, and saies further, that the
said James Bowen was in a deplorable condition and he believed
perished by extreme Cold and Hunger.
Sworn as above

3 Feb. 1740
before me.   William Charlwood,   Joseph Godding
                         Coroner.

Hopkins Switzer being Sworne proved the same.

From *Surrey Record Office KE3/1/101.* 1739–40.

document

Settlement litigation, 1815

I spent several hours at the Clerkenwell Sessions. A case came
before the court ludicrous because of the minuteness required
in the examination. Was the pauper settled in parish A or B?
The house he occupied was in both parishes, and models
both of the house and of the bed in which the pauper slept were
laid before the Court that it might ascertain how much of his
body lay in each parish. The Court held the pauper to be
settled where his head (being the nobler part) lay, though one
of his legs at least, and great part of his body, lay out of the
parish.

From the *Diary, Reminiscences and Correspondence of Henry Crabb
Robinson*, ed. Thomas Sadler, 3rd ed., 1872, quoted in (**47**).

II. MANAGING THE POOR

document 4

Role of overseers

Dr Burn wrote with a legal and sympathetic understanding of the practical difficulties facing the overseers: his 'The Justice of the Peace and the Parish Officer' *was their primary work of reference. This passage explains the onerous tasks which fell to unpaid citizens, and why the gentry took so jaundiced a view of appointment to the office.*

To keep an extraordinary look-out, to prevent persons coming to inhabit without certificates, and to fly to the justices to remove them; and if a man brings a certificate, then to caution all the inhabitants not to let him a farm of £10 a year, and to take care to keep him out of all parish offices: To warn them, if they will hire servants, to hire them half-yearly, or by the month, by the week, or by the day, rather than by any way that shall give them a settlement; or if they do hire them for a year, then to endeavour to pick a quarrel with them before the year's end, and so get rid of them. To maintain their poor as cheap as possibly they can at all events; not to lay out two-pence in prospect of any future good, but only to serve the present necessity: To bargain with some sturdy person to take them by the lump, who yet is not intended to take them, but to hang over them *in terrorem* if they shall complain to the justices for want of maintenance. . . . To bind out poor children apprentices, no matter to whom, or to what trade, but to take especial care that the master live in another parish; To move heaven and earth, if any dispute happens about a settlement: and in that particular, to invert the general rule, and stick at no expence: To pull down cottages: To drive out as many inhabitants, and admit as few, as possible; that is to depopulate the parish in order to lessen the Poor Rate: To be generous indeed, sometimes, in giving a portion, with the mother of a bastard child, to the reputed father, on condition that he will marry her; or with a poor widow; always provided that the husband is settled elsewhere: or if a poor man, with a large family, appears to be industrious, *overseers* will charitably assist him in taking a farm in some *neighbouring parish*, and give him £10 to pay his first year's rent with: And if any one of their poor has a mercantile genius, they will purchase for him a box, with pins, needles, laces, buckles, and such like wares, and send him abroad in the quality of a petty chapman; with the profits thereof, and a moderate hunch at stealing, he can decently support himself, and educate his children in the same *industrious* way—But to see that the Poor shall report to church, and bring their children there to be instructed; to contract with a master, that he shall procure apprentice at proper times to be taught to read or write; to provide a stock of materials to set the Poor on work; to see the aged and impotent comfortably sustained; the sick healed; and all of them cloathed with neatness and decency: These, in such like, it is to be feared, are not so generally regarded, as the laws intended, and *the necessity of the case requires*

From R. Burn (**83**).

document 5

Appointment of overseers

To the High Constables of the Hundreds of Copthorne and Effingham in the County of Surrey.

These are to command You to give immediate Notice to all and every the Overseers of the Poor of their said several Parishes that they make out a list in writing of a competent number of substantial Householders within their respective Districts and deliver in the same to his Majesty's Justices of the Peace for the said County at the Coffee House in Epsom . . . to the end that out of the said List the said Justices may appoint other Overseers of the Poor for the Year then next ensuing.

From *Surrey Quarter Sessions Papers.*
QS 21/20. 1759–64.

document 6

Expenses of parish officers' elections
At St Lawrence, Winchester, 1766.

April 4 At choyce of New Officers at the Whit Hart:
A Ham, Fowls, quarter of Lamb, Salets, Appel Pyes, Bread Butter and Chees all included £1. 5. 0., Beer £0. 8. 5., Punch

£1. 4. 0., Rumbo £0. 2. 6. 3 Dozen and one Bottles of Wine £3. 14. 0. Fier £0. 4. 0. Tobacco £0. 2. 6. 8 Glass Broke £0. 4. 0.

£7. 4. 5.

From W. E. Tate (40)

document 7

Abuse of contracting

This document illustrates well the malpractice which commonly arose from the technique of contracting.

The Governor of the workhouse contracts with Grimsby and the other parishes who send their poor there, to clothe and fee the inmates for three shillings a head (per week), at all ages from birth, he having the benefit of the work of all those able to earn anything towards their support. The person who at present fills this office is an elderly single man, of irregular and dirty habits; and from want of attention on the part of the parochial authorities, not the slightest attention is paid either to classification, discipline, cleanliness, or even to separation of the sexes. I found the whole house in a filthy condition, with all the paupers huddled together in the kitchen over the fire; the lodging rooms ill-ventilated, each pauper keeping the key of the room in which himself and his family slept. Egress and ingress to the house free to all. The inmates full of complaints respecting their treatment, either by the governor or the parish. . . . Another inmate was an unfortunate idiot lad of about nineteen or twenty. I was shown the sleeping place of this poor wretch in an outhouse in the yard, with a very damp brick floor, half of which had been pulled up; his bed a heap of filthy litter, with a miserable rug full of holes for covering; his clothing, though in the middle of winter, consisted of nothing but a long shirt of sacking; and a leather strap with a chain fastened to the wall was in the corner, to make him fast when he was unruly. The whole presented a spectacle alike disgraceful to a civilised country and to the parish where it exists.

From *Report of Poor Law Inquiry Commissioners*, 1833. Wylde's *Report*, Appendix A, pp. 134-5.

Workhouse Rules

These additional rules were established for the government of the Wimbledon Workhouse, 1775.

The mistress or matron is to rise early and to appear soon after in a decent clean dress among the poor under her management and to see that the orders and directions prescribed for their conduct be duly observed, taking care to behave with kindness and tenderness towards them and to avoid all hasty and passionate language, particularly calling any of the poor by harsh or reproachful names, on every occasion.

No poor person is to send for medicines or goods of any kind whatsoever to be brought to the workhouse, all which are to be ordered by the churchwardens or overseers or by the matron under their direction.

Upon any debate or noise they are every one of them immediately to become silent at the order of the matron and not to contradict her upon any occasion, taking care to avoid indecent and abusive language and all mocking and scoffing at each other, but upon any ground of complaint they may lay the same before one of the churchwardens or overseers.

Such of the poor as shall be guilty of any of the offences above mentioned shall be debarred by the matron from their next meal and where the offence is such as ought not to be lightly passed over immediate complaint shall be made thereof by the matron to the overseers who shall cause the offender to be duly punished without delay.

. . . Such poor persons (admitted) shall at their admission, or as soon after as possible, deliver up all their goods and effects to the overseers for the benefit of the parish, and they are not to have any box, drawer, or other receptacle under lock and key, but may each of them receive from the matron a proper box belonging to the workhouse with a lid thereto for holding their linen and wearing apparel, which boxes are to be continually open to the inspection of the matron whenever she thinks proper

All poor persons are diligently to perform to the utmost of their power any work allotted to them. . . .

The churchwardens and overseers are admonished and warned not to relieve any persons admitted to the workhouse . .

except such as wear upon the shoulder of the right sleeve of their uppermost garment a badge as prescribed by the Act of 8 & 9 William 3 cap. 30. . . .

The foregoing rules written in a fair legible hand are to be affixed in a conspicuous place in the workhouse and the same are to be publicly read by the matron on the first Sunday in every month, or oftener if she shall see fit, to the poor under her management.

From *Wimbledon Vestry Minutes*, Surrey Record Society, vol. 25.

document 9

Workhouse costs

The initial saving of the workhouse experiment is apparent in this table, as is its long-term inadequacy in diminishing costs.

Name	Opening date	Cost before opening	Cost after opening yr		1776	1783	1785
		£		£	£	£	£
St Andrews Holland	1727	1,000	1730	750	1,329	1,538	1,589
St Giles-in-the Fields	1726	—	1727	903	5,156	5,195	6,232
St Paul's Bedford	—	300 about	1721	197	716	830	837
Westham Essex	1726	460	1727	230	1,707	2,509	2,899
Hemel Hempstead Herts	1720	730	1722	388	822	858	966
Maidstone	1720	929	1724	53	1,555	2,251	2,271
Stroud	1730 (pre)	230	1730	115	429	495	495
Tonbridge	1726	570		380	1,114	1,365	1,695
Harborough Leics	1722	170		100	314	478	351
Peterborough	1724	499		334	919	910	905
Chertsey, Surrey	1727	607	1728	395	758	1,271	972
Bradford, Wilts	1727	7–800	1731	400	1,775 2,815	—	2,415

From F. M. Eden, (**92**).

An early instance of contracting for the poor

Advertisement for a contractor in the *Northampton Mercury*, 29 March 1749.

To be Lett, And Enter'd upon immediately—The Poor of the Parish of Eaton Socon, in the County of Bedfordshire, to be maintained and cloathed in a decent and proper manner. Any person, that is willing to take the same, is desired to direct a letter to Mr Edward Pridmore, Overseer of the Poor in the said Parish; who is empowered to treat with him for the same.

N.B. There is a convenient and proper House, in good Repair, with an Orchard well-planted with Fruit Trees, and a Piece of Ground contiguous to the same, proper for a Garden.

From F. G. Emisson, (**61**).

Advertisement for a Workhouse Master

Parish of St Mary le Bone, in the county of Middlesex, Sept. 7 1768.

WANTED, A MASTER of the WORKHOUSE, capable of instructing and employing the poor of the said parish in some useful work or manufacture. Any person or persons who think themselves qualified for the office, must bring sufficient testimony of their character, skill, and ability, to the said Workhouse, in Paddington-street, on Wednesday the 21st instant, at eleven o'clock in the forenoon.

From A. R. Neate (**69**).

Relief assessment

This overseer's report shows the 'fatal tendencies of Speenhamland' in doling relief beyond the needs or desires of the poor.

		Actual allowance demanded by the poor	Justices allowance according to families' size	Difference	
1.	W.E.	6. 4. 2.	7. 6. 1.	1. 1. 11.	
2.	G.S.	7. 10. 0.	13. 13. 3.	6. 3. 3.	
3.	T.H.	2. 17. 0.	6. 8. 9.	3. 11. 9.	
4.	T.W.	2. 2. 0.	3. 7. 9.	1. 5. 9.	
5.	T.B.	3. 3. 0.	6. 8. 5.	3. 5. 5.	
				15. 8. 1.	Total for five families

From F. M. Eden (**92**).

document 13

Comment on Pitt's Poor Bill

Pitt's Poor Bill was circulated for comment, and these three observations demonstrate stock reactions:

(a) From Mr Ellis, Clerk of the Peace for Sussex, 3 February 1797

. . . I have every day before me the evils that arise from poore children being kept at home with their parents they there imbibe a Habit of Indolence as they grow up . . . I lately also saw a young girl brought to a workhouse by her Parents that was 18 years of age who would not do any species of work whatever, I have also seen in a number of instances where paupers have from 4 to 8 and ten children and asked relief and the Overseers have desired them to send some of their children into a House of Industry . . . they have refused and will almost starve sooner than comply.

(b) From Mr Robson, Curate of Whitechapel, 9 February 1797

Sir,
    Permit me, in the name of numberless poor Persons, to thank you for your endeavours to ameliorate their Condition.

A powerful opposition, however, is forming against the Bill which you have formed. Several Parishes co-operate with these of Bloomsbury and St Giles, in concerting measures to defeat it. The Dread of increase Expense operates on the minds of the Vestrymen, and the Bulk of the Magistrates. . . .

(Mr Robson appends a 'little Paper' outlining a plan for dealing with the poor.)
PRO 30/8/308

(c) From Rev. C. V. Michell. To the Rt. Hon.ble. William Pitt, July 9th, 1797

Sir,
. . . Having for some years been Curate of the Parish from wh. I date this letter, I have continually attended to the necessities of the poor, and the unfeeling conduct of the Parish Officers. Often have I wish'd for an opportunity of conversing with men, whose situation in life gives them a Power of enacting whatever may be beneficial, and abolishing whatever is oppressive . . . (one or two circumstances, however, still remain strongly impressed on my mind) . . . the Overseers of the Poor are illiterate men, frequently hard-hearted and unfeeling; for the most approv'd are those who save most for the Parish. When it falls to the Lot of a gentleman to come into Office, a Hireling presents himself who, for a few guineas, takes upon him to pinch the poor. How this circumstance can be remedied I cannot ascertain.

The Parish Meetings are attended by none, but those of a similar description to the Overseer. The business, as far as relates to the Payment of the Poor, is settled without opposition. If the poor complain to a magistrate, in some way or other, they are persecuted for it. . . .

> C. V. MICHELL,
> Weston-under-Penyard, near Ross, Herefordshire.

From *The Chatham Papers.*

Distribution of food

The magistracy was forced by extreme food shortage to regulate distribution to the poor. They were not directed in this procedure by the central government. The following instruction was addressed to the overseer of the poor.

Totmonslow North, Staffordshire.

Whereas by an Act of Parliament, passed in the last Session entitled 'an Act for making better Provision for the maintenance of the Poor; and for diminishing the consumption of Bread Corn &c. &c.' The Magistrates, or any two or more of them are requested at their Petty Sessions, by any writing under their Hands and Seals to order the Overseers of the Poor of every Parish, Township, or Place within the respective Division for which they act, within a time fixed in such order to provide a sufficient Stock of such Provision as the Magistrates shall Chuse (other than and except Wheaten Bread, or the kind of bread in common use in such Divisions) to be distributed the same as they shall also direct, according to the said Act. We Edward Powys Clerk, and W. H. Coyny Esquire, two of his Majesty's Justices of the Peace for the County of Stafford, at our Petty Sessions, held the 16th February 1801, at the House of Wm. Brough, the Red Lion in Leek, do hereby order you to provide within a Fortnight from the date hereof, a sufficient Stock of Rice, so as to give the Poor within your District, who are ordered to receive weekly pay, one fourth of such weekly pay in Rice, after the rate of Sixpence a Pound. And that you attend at the House of the said William Brough, in Leek aforesaid, on Easter Monday, the 6th. of April next, to give an account to the Magistrates there assembled what you have done herein. Fail not, under a heavy Penalty, inflicted by the said Act of Parliament.

N.B. An Inspector will be appointed at the next Petty Sessions. Given under our Hands and Seals this 16th. February, 1801.

(signed) EDWARD POWYS

W. H. COYNY

From the *County Record Office, Stafford.* Q/SB A 1801.

Badging the Poor

Badging the Poor sought to identify, and to stigmatise, the pauper. The provision here recorded is a sad one, signifying the harsh attitudes which stemmed from mercantilist needs to utilise the labour force.

'From 1 September 1697 Person and Wife and Children co-habiting in the same House shall upon the Shoulder of the right Sleeve of the uppermost Garment . . . in an open and visible manner wear such Badge or Mark . . . a large Roman P, together with the first Letter of Name of Parish . . . cut either in red or blew Cloth. . . .

From 'An Act for Supplying some Defects in the Laws for the Relief of the Poor of this Kingdom', 1696/1697, *State Papers*.

Almshouses

A plaque on a cottage wall at Strand-on-the-Green, Chiswick, demonstrates continuation of charitable activity in the period between the Restoration and the new humanitarianism after 1750.

B. HOPKINS MORRIS
Homes of Rest 1933
Trustees of Chiswick Parochial Charities
Repaird 1816
J^as. Wilson   Churchwardens
W^m. Wallis Bifield

Two of these Houses built by R. Thomas Child one by M. Solomon Williams one by William Abbot Carpinter at his own Charge for yuse of Poor of Chiswick forever.

1704

Particularity of donations

Particularity of donations was a characteristic of posthumous charity. This fund still exists.

THE HOPKINS CHARITY
Established in Wednesbury, Staffs., on 7 April 1681, giving £200 to be laid out in lands and tenements in or near Wednesbury. . . .
'. . . to dispose of in the yearly providing for and bestowing upon such *three poor men* and such *three poor women*, inhabitants of Wednesbury, as . . . *good new woollen cloth coats and gowns* . . . to be delivered yearly on St Thomas' Day in the Parish Church of Wednesbury, after Divine Service . . . to bestow residue of rents in *bread and money* amongst the other poor inhabitants. . . .'

From a Government Report of 1823.

105

Quantification

Gregory King's estimate of the numbers and incomes of different classes, 1688, was the first attempt at numerical assessment of the poor. This abbreviated form indicates the overwhelming size of the problem as contemporaries saw it.

	No. of families	Ranks, degrees, titles and qualifications	Heads per family (household)	No. of persons	Yearly income/ family
I	511,586	Temporal lords, merchants, clergy, farmers, shopkeepers, military officers, etc.	5¼	2,675,520	67
II	50,000	Common seamen	3	150,000	20
	364,000	Labouring people and out servants	3½	1,275,000	15
II	400,000	Cottagers and paupers	3¼	1,300,000	6·10
	35,000	Common soldiers	2	70,000	14
	849,000	Vagrants	3¼	2,795,000	10·10
				30,000	
	849,000		3¼	2,825,000	10·10

I 'Increasing the wealth of the kingdom'.........2,675,520   67
II 'Decreasing the wealth of the kingdom'........2,825,000   10·10
1,360,586..............Nett Totals...................5,500,520   32

From 'Natural and Political Observations and conclusions upon the State and Condition of England', published in G. Chalmers's *An Estimate of the Comparative Strength of Great Britain*, 1804 ed.

Population growth and poor rates

This table of relative population growth and amount of poor rates in England and Wales is only accurate beyond 1801, but it illustrates

*how beguiling Malthus's interpretation must have seemed, and also
the reservation held during the mid-1820s.*

A.D.	Population	Amount of Poor Rate £	Per Head s.	Wheat/Quarter s.
1660	5,500,000			
1688	5,500,000	Nearly 700,000	2/6	
1701		Nearly 900,000		
1714	5,750,000	950,000	3/6¾	
1760	7,000,000	1,250,000		
1776		1,529,780		
1780	8,000,000			
1784		2,004,238	5/0¼	
1801	9,172,980			
1803	9,210,000	4,077,891	8/10¼	
1813	10,505,800	6,656,106	12/8	108/9
1818	11,876,200	7,870,801	13/3	84/1
1824	12,517,900	5,736,900	9/2	62/–
1832	14,105,600	7,036,969	10/–	63/4
1834	14,372,000	6,317,255	8/9½	51/11

From G. Nicholls (**36**).

document 20

Education

*The number of children educated in England and Wales, in endowed and
non-endowed schools, in 1819, suggests the possibility of wide literacy,
capable of absorbing the radical press of the 1820s.*

	Endowed schools			Unendowed schools			Sunday schools	
	No. of schools	No. of children	Total revenues	Dames' schools	Total schools	No. of children	No. of schools	No. of children
England	4,167	165,433	£300,000	3,102	14,282	478,849	5,162	452,817
Wales	209	7,625	£5,817	73	572	22,976	301	24,408

From the Returns of Brougham's Select Committee of 1818
Parliamentary Papers 1820, vol. 12, pp. 342–55).

*The following family budgets are taken from geographically dispara:
regions and further illustrate the plight of working men in the period (
the French Wars.*

1. *A cooper from Frome, Somerset*, aged 50, with wife and fiv
children.

Income £63.14s./an. (employing his own two youngest childre
aged 11 and 7).
Expenses. £100.2s./8d. . . . aided by free fuel from his trade
diet including butter, cheese, sugar, tea, meat and milk.

2. *Agricultural labour from Presteigne in Radnorshire*, aged 40, wit
a wife and five children under ten years old.
Earnings 6/–/week—first relief from parish in 1794–1795.
Occasional income from his wife's baking.
Expenses. Half a bushel of wheat per week cost 6/–.
House rent was 30/– a year.
The family breakfasted on 'onion pottage', and had bread (
potatoes for dinner and supper. Very rarely was meat or butt
eaten. The poor were 'literally starving in Presteigne, 1793
1794'.

3. *A carter from Manchester*, aged 39, with a wife and seve
children.
Income amounted to £44.4s., helped by elder girls nursing f
neighbours, and his wife's 6d./week for roving cotton.
Expenditure, £47./16s., including 2/–/week for rent. Th
family ate oatmeal bread, but a varied diet, which includ
meat, potatoes, tea and sugar, milk, cheese, and butter.

4. *A miner from Nent Head in Cumberland*, aged 45, with a wi
and seven children.
Earnings £26 from his efforts, £18 from his wife and childrer
washing—a total of £44.
Expenses. £3./an. in rent. Barley bread, potatoes, oatmeal. N
wheat bread, but milk, cheese, meat (£10 a year) and tea ar
sugar. £2 on soap and candles.

4. *A miner from Sunderland*, aged 45, with wife and three girls.
Income. Paid to his master for rent and fuel, and was left with
£29./18s. The family was 'given' £5./5s.
Expenses. Bread meal was allowed by the mines' owner at 1/6 a
stone. No wheat, butter, or beer; but tea, and milk, and meat.
Soap accounted for 19/9 a year. Other items included the
maintenance of his wife's bastard, born before his marriage
and wear and tear of work gear.
Despite periodic sickness, this miner had no relief from the
parish.

5. *A labourer from Banbury, Oxon*, widower of mid-50's, three
children, 21, 13, and 7 years old.
Earnings 8/- a week for 48 weeks; 9/- in summer months.
Eldest daughter sickly, kept home, but second girl at school,
where provided with clothes. Parish allowed father 2/- a week
for children, making for a total income of £26./4s.
Expenses. £13./13s./an. on wheat bread, and diet included
bacon, tea, sugar, butter and milk, but in small quantities. The
man was in debt, and clearly relied on neighbours, who provided him and his family with old clothes. He was also helped
by the 3 or 4 bushells of potatoes which were produced from
160 sq. yds. of garden.

7. *A labourer of Kendal, Westmorland*, 29 years old, with a wife
and three children, aged 4, 2, and 1.
Earnings £29./19s., including his wife's small income for wind-
ing.
Expenses. Budget balanced, with very little spent on meat and
flour (oatmeal provided the staple). But he bought 40 lbs. of
butter a year, and spent the large sum of £3./10s. on fuel.
'Not a shilling in the ale house'.

8. *A labourer from Ealing, Middlesex*, aged 29, with a wife and
four children.
Income. £38./12s.—supplemented by wife's earnings during
harvest.
Expenses. Paid £3./18s. for his cottage and garden. Ate wheat
bread (a quartern loaf per day), and this, with meat, cheese
and small beer made up his diet. His two eldest children (both
boys) learned to read at 3d. each.

109

Relied also on perquisites of vegetables from his master'
garden, and a quart of skim milk every monrning. Outgoing
totaled £39./0s./4d., and he 'complains heavily' and asks fo
wage increase.

From F. M. Eden (**92**).

Grain and Spirit production

The output of British spirits shows a certain correlation with whea
prices. The high period of gin-drinking is one of high grain yield, th
proposition being that surplus cereal resulted in greater drink, rathe
than food, consumption. The parliamentary Act of 1751 is seen to hav
had a dramatic effect, despite the temporary continuation of favourabl
harvests.

Date	Output of spirits mill.galls	Wheat prices S./qtr.
1705	1·44	23
1710	2·20	60
1720	2·48	34
1725	3·93	47
1730	3·78	34
1735	6·44	36
1740	6·65	45
1745	7·20	25
1750	6·61	31
1755	4·65	29
1760	2·32	30
1765	2·23	45
1770	2·57	40
1775	2·51	46
1780	2·72	34
1785	3·14	54
1790	4·32	58
1795	5·15	92
1800	4·84	128

From T. S. Ashton (**1**).

Personal Possessions

The few possessions of the poor can be studied minutely from inventories, made by the overseers when a person was about to be admitted to the workhouse.

An Inventory of Wid. Brooks's goods taken 21 June 1748.

A cupboard with 2 doors; 1 old table; 1 chair; 1 box; 1 stool; 1 bed and bedstead; clothing to do.; 1 table; 1 pail; 1 cupboard.

1 March 1752
Whereas Wid. Beakes has been in person and made complaint for relief and desired a pension, which was granted and a room allowed her in the parish houses and by the desire of the parishioners the officers have this day taken an inventory of her goods, but she says she will sooner go a-begging about the country than live in the parish house, it is agreed that she shall not have any relief until she condescends to the order of the vestry.

The Inventory of Goods

One chest of drawers; a bed and bedstead, 5 chairs, 2 joint stools; 3 pewter dishes and 3 plates; 1 Delf dish, 5 earthen plates; 1 trunk, 1 table, 1 pr. of bellows; 1 warming pan, 2 porridge pots; 2 pictures, 16 cups and saucers, 3 tea-pots.

From *The Wimbledon Vestry Minutes, 1743–1788*, Surrey Record Society, vol. 25.

Provision of accommodation

Cottage building was generally discouraged, but the settled poor were provided with accommodation before the workhouse came to offer an alternative roof.

1667.
Robert Wheeler a poor Inhabitant of East Betchworth, 'is destitute of a habitacion, his house being lately blowne and

fallen downe', and is in the charge of the parish. Ordered that, at the instance of the Churchwardens and Overseers of the parish, they may erect a cottage on the waste of the Manor of East Betchworth, with the consent of Sir Ralph Freeman, lord of the Manor, for the habitacion of the said Wheeler: the same cottage to be hereafter continued for the use of the poor of the parish.

From *Surrey Quarter Sessions Order Book, 1666–68,* vol. 9, pp. 22. Issued by Surrey County Council 1951.

IV. CHILDREN OF THE POOR

document 25

Bastardy

The bastard took the place in which he was born as his place of settlement, but it was clearly in the interest of the parish to establish paternity for the support of the illegitimate child. The case of Rose Cradock is interesting because the accusation below was followed by a second, against one Robert Sturgeon, servant to a Chelsea pastrycook, but again involving the fishmonger Mr Sam. Gilbert. The colourful circumstances of conception contrast with a later reference to the birth: 'delivered in the workhouse on the 20th of August'.

The Voluntary Examination of Rose Cradock Spinster.

This Examinant saith on her Oath that she was born in the Parish of St Luke Chelsea in the County of Middlesex and that she is about seventeen years of age. . . .

This Examinant further saith that she never was married and that she is now pregnant of an illegitimate child or children unlawfully begotten on her body by one James Morris, an a Prentice to Mr Price shoemaker in Chelsea aforesaid who had Carnal knowledge of her Body several times in the house of Mr Sam. Gilbert a fishmonger in Chelsea aforesaid—and that the said James Morris is the real and true father of the child or children she is now pregnant with, and no man else. And this Examinant further saith that she is about seven months advanced in her pregnancy and that the said Bastard child or

children when born is or are likely to become chargable to the
Parish of Chelsea aforesaid.

her

Rose × Cradock

mark

Sworn before me one of his Majesty's
Justices of the Peace in and for the
County of Middlesex June 15: 1784 (signed)
From *Greater London Record Office P74/LUK/123.*

document 26

A shotgun marriage

*A putative father was in no position to argue his innocence. Mere
accusation was sufficient for the poor law officials to insist on his forcible,
but legal, betrothal.*

25 Jan 1787.
Rode to Ringland this Morning and married one Robert Astick
and Elizabeth Howlett by Licence . . . and the Man being in
Custody, the Woman being with Child by him. The Man was
a long time before he could be prevailed on to marry her when
in the Church Yard; and at the Altar behaved very unbecoming.
It is a cruel thing that any Person should be compelled by Law
to marry. I recd. of the Officers for marrying them 0.10.6. It
is very disagreeable to me to marry such Persons.

From *Parson Woodforde's Diary* (**112**).

document 27

Indenture of an apprentice

*Girls were bound into domestic service as drudges, and in this case no
indication of any specific training is given. It typifies the decline of
apprenticeship, the vanished requirement to provide specific instruction.*

North Riding of the County of York.

This INDENTURE made the seventh day of August in the year
of Our Lord 1804, Between Michael Glenton and Robert Ward
being the Major part of the Churchwardens and Overseers of
the Poor of the Township of Wensley in the said Riding and

Margaret Spensley a poor child of the said township on the one part, and Robert Sweten of Barnard Castle in the County of Durham Weaver, on the other part, WITNESSETH, that the said Churchwardens and Overseers of the Poor have, by & with the Consent Allowance and Approbation of two of his Majesty's Justices of the Peace for the said North Riding put, placed, & bound the said Margaret Spensley as an apprentice to, & with the said Robert Sweten with him to dwell & remain from the Day of the Date hereof until the said Apprentice shall attain the age of Twenty one years, or Marriage according to the form of the statute made in that case and provided. During all which said Term her said Master well and truly shall serve, his Secrets shall keep his Commands (being lawful and honest) at all times willingly shall perform; and in all things as a good and faithful servant shall demean herself towards her said Master and all his family. And the said Robert Sweten, for himself, his Executors, Administrators and assigns, doth Covenant Promise and Agree to & with the said Churchwardens, Overseers, & his said Apprentice, that he will educate & bring her up on some honest & lawful calling, & in the fear of God . . . & that he will find, provide for & allow unto his said Apprentice sufficient wholesome and competent Meat, Drink, Washing, Lodging, Apparel and all other Necessaries meet for such an Apprentice during the said Term. Provided always that the said last mentioned Covenant on the part of the said Robert Sweten, his Executors and Administrators to be done and performed shall continue and be in force for no longer than for three Calender Months next after the death of the said Robert Sweten in case he the said Robert Sweten shall happen to die during the continuance of such apprenticeship according to the provisions of an Act passed in the 32nd. year of the reign of King George the Third intitled, An Act for the further regulation of Parish Apprentices.

In witness thereoff the said parties to these Present have hereunto interchargeably set their Hands and Seals the Day and Year first above written

        (signed) Michael Glenton, Churchwarden
        Robert Ward, Overseers of the Poor
        Robert Sweten, Master

Sealed and delivered in the presence of
                    Wm. Ridley
                    Paul Greathead (signed)
Allowed by us, two of his Majesty's Justices of the Peace for
the said North Riding
                    Wm. Chaytor
                    Wm. Chaytor, Junr.

From E. Trotter (45).

An absconded apprentice
document 28

Whereas Samuel Haycox, Apprentice to John Mansell, Rule-
Maker, in Wolverhampton, did, on Wednesday the 16th. Inst.
elope from the Service of his said Master, this is to forewarn all
Persons from harbouring or employing; for as he has been
repeatedly guilty of Misdemeanors, if they do, they will be
proceeded against as the Law directs. He is about Five Feet,
three or four Inches high, dark brown Hair, a little in natural
curl, fair Complexion, blubber-cheeked, gray Eyes, crook-
Knee'd, and full Shouldered. Had on when he went away, a
blue Frize, or brown cloth-coloured Coat, and soiled Leather
Breeches.
Whoever will secure him and give Notice to his said Master, so
that he may be brought to Justice, shall receive Half a Guinea
Reward, to be paid by me,

JOHN MANSELL

From *Aris's Birmingham Gazette*, 21 May 1770.

Factory Children
document 29

*Evidence given to the Sadler Committee on Factory Children's Labour.
1831–1832.*

Samuel Coulson on his own children.

Question. At what time in the morning, in the brisk time, did those girls go to the mills?

Answer. In the brisk time, for about six weeks, they have gone at 3 o'clock in the morning, and ended at 10, or nearly half past at night.

Q. What intervals were allowed for rest or refreshment during those nineteen hours of labour?

A. Breakfast, a quarter of an hour, and dinner half an hour, and drinking a quarter of an hour.

Q. Was any of that time taken up in cleaning the machinery?

A. They generally had to do what they call dry down; sometimes this took the whole of the time at breakfast or drinking, and they were to get their dinner or breakfast as they could; if not, it was brought home.

Q. Had you not great difficulty in awakening your children to this excessive labour?

A. Yes, in the early time we had them to take up asleep and shake them, when we got them on the floor to dress them, before we could get them off to work; but not so in the common hours. . . .

Q. What was the length of time they could be in bed during those long hours?

A. It was near 11 o'clock before we could get them into bed after getting a little victuals, and then at morning my mistress used to stop up all night, for fear that we could not get them ready for the time; sometimes we have gone to bed, and one of us generally awoke.

Q. What time did you get them up in the morning?

A. In general me or my mistress got up at 2 o'clock to dress them.

Q. So that they had not above four hours' sleep at this time? . . .

A. Yes.

Q. Were the children excessively fatigued by this labour?

A. Many times; we have cried often when we have given them the little victualling we had to give them; we had to shake them, and they have fallen asleep with the victuals in their mouths many a time.'

From *Parliamentary Papers, 1831–32*, vol. 25.

116

The Child Sweep

Letter XIV   to Rt. Hon. Lord Mayor of London and the
                           Magistrates of London and Westminster.

My Lord and Gentlemen,
I have now before my eyes a particular object of the misery I
have endeavoured to describe. The object in question . . . is
now twelve years of age, a cripple on crutches, hardly three feet
seven inches in stature. He began to climb chimnies *before*
he was five years of age, his bones not having acquired a fit
degree of strength. In consequence of his treatment, his legs
and feet resemble an S more than an L. His hair felt like hog's
bristles, and his head like a warm cinder. He was once *blind*
for six months, but still he did his work. Notwithstanding his
arduous contest with nature for life and scanty bread, what
attention has been shown him?—Being out of his time of
servitude, as a *reward* for his labours and sufferings, he is become
an object of the parochial charity. . . .
It is the custom of the trade of chimney sweepers to enter into
a second seven years indenture; but in the maimed condition of
this poor boy, it is to be hardly expected of the virtue of chimney
sweepers, that one will take the crippled leavings of another . . .
being asked if ever went to church, his answer was 'I have no
hat for my head, no buckles for my shoes.' He had no cap but
that in which he climbed chimnies: this they usually pull over
their faces to guard their eyes. His parish coat was whole; and
he reported that he had one shirt beside his climbing ragged
dress.
This boy . . . still performs his duty to his mistress; and though
he cannot move on the surface of the earth without the assistance of crutches, and has aid from the parish, he climbs and
sweeps the chimney. He must necessarily depend on his hands
and knees . . . it is wonderful that every boy . . . is not crippled.
They are generally bandy-leg'd. Beginning to climb before the
bone has acquired a solidity, the daily pressure necessarily gives
the leg a twist if it does not distort the ankles.
By the benignity of some true christian ladies of this neigh-
bourhood, this boy stands a fair chance of being put into some

other way of life ... rescued from the iron claws of cruelty ...
a monument of reproach to those in whose hands he has been
sorely treated. ...

I am, & c.,

J.H.

From Jonas Hanway, *A Sentimental History of Chimney Sweepers*,
1785.

The infant parish poor

... Many children instead of being nourished with care, by the
fostering hand or breast of a wholesome country nurse, and
thrust into the impure air of a workhouse, into the hands of
some careless, worthless young female, or decrepid old woman,
and inevitably lost for want of such means as the God of nature,
their father as well as ours, has appointed for *their* preservation.

It is hard to say, how many lives these cities have lost, or how
many they yet loose annually, by the poverty, filth, and vice of
parents, which no public institutions in this land of freedom
can save; and tho' we live on as fine a spot as any of the three
kingdoms can boast of, yet by being closely built, and many
living in confined places, and many too much congregated,
joined to the sulphureous air created by so vast a number of coal
fires, we must not be surprised, that so great a proportion as
20,232 in 43,101, or near 47 per cent. die under 2 years of age:
this appears by an account now before me of 1756, 1757, and
1758. At these times the Foundling Hospital was open for in-
discriminate reception; consequently the mortality there not
being comprehended in the bills of mortality, rendered those
bills so much the lighter. ...

As far as I can trace out the evil, there has been such devasta-
tion ... for half a century past, that at a moderate computation
1,000 or 1,200 children have annually perished, under the
direction of the parish officers. I say under their direction, not
that they ordered them to be *killed*; but that they *did not order*
such means to be used, as are necessary to keep them *alive*.
How will this stand recorded in our annals!

. . . another parish, some years before the Foundling Hospital was opened, wherein it appeared, that of 54 children born, and taken into their workhouse, not one out-lived the year in which it was born or taken in. This seemed to be so incredible, that I went to the workhouse to enquire into the fact, and found it true. The workhouse was airy and well situated; but *such was their nursing*!

From Jonas Hanway (**98**).

document 32
Whiston on charity schools: a sermon

A CHARITY SERMON PREACHED AT TRINITY CHURCH, CAMBRIDGE, JANUARY 25, 1705.

At which Time and Place the several Teachers of the Charity Schools, lately erected in *Cambridge* appear'd, with the POOR CHILDREN under their Care, in Number about *Three Hundred*.
To which is added
A Particular Account of the Said *Charity Schools*.
By William WHISTON, M.A., Professor of the Mathematicks in the University of Cambridge.
2 Tim.III.15.
And that from a Child thou hast known the Holy Scripture, which are able to make thee wise unto salvation, through faith which is in Christ Jesus.
III. The Proper and Peculiar Time for the attaining of this Divine Knowledge is Infancy and Childhood, or as soon as even the capacity of Children will admit of Instruction. For this is set down here as the great Commendation of *Timothy*, the great Reason of his extraordinary Proficiency. . . . Now the great Usefulness and Necessity of this way of Education of Poor Children will appear, if we consider
1. That this way of Education of Poor Children, will contribute mightily to their own and others Welfare and Happiness, even in this World.
2. That if Poor Children be not thus taught and instructed when they are Young, they must in all Probability . . . *perish* for ever for lack of Knowledge.

119

3. That if they be not brought under the York of Order and Discipline when they are Young they will usually be too obstinate in Vice and Wicked Customs to be ever after dissuaded from them, and so perish also for ever in their open wickedness.

4. That this way of Education of Poor Children will prevent their falling into many and dangerous Temptations afterward

5. That this way of Education of Poor Children, if once spread through the Nation, would mightily prevent or cure the sad and unhappy Schisms and Division of this Church and Kingdom, which are so Fatal, and threaten so great Ruin to Both.

And O that now, for a conclusion, I could prevail with those who are Rich in this World, *to do good, to be rich in good works to be ready to distribute, willing to communicate; laying up in store for themselves a good foundation against their time to come, that they may lay hold on Eternal Life!* . . . It being, I think, very demonstrable the one Twentieth part of what we now annually tax ourselve for the Publick Occasion of War and Defence, if once settled and rightley and prudently managed, would provide for the Education of all the Poorest Children of this Nation, and do somewhat considerable towards the Clothing of a great part of them . . . that the Poor Children of this place in the future . . shall . . . have ever reason to *rise up and call* their Benefactor *blessed.* . . . While the Contributors also themselves . . . have been faithful over a few things, I will make you rulers over many things . . . inherit the Kingdom prepared for you from the foundation of the World: For I was an hungered, and ye gave me meat; and I was thirsty, and ye gave me drink; and I was a stranger, and ye took me in; naked, and ye clothed me. . . Verily I say unto you, inasmuch as ye have done it unto one of the least of these my Brethren, ye have done it unto me.

From *Charity Sermons:* British Museum.

document 3

Education and establishments

This contribution to the debate in the House of Lords on Whitbread's Parochial Schools Bill, 11 August 1807, looks damaging to the moder view, and presages the insularity of the denominations and nineteenth-century educational progress. (The intention was to establish a school in every parish, to be maintained by the rates.)

The Archbishop of Canterbury trusted he should not be considered hostile to the principle of diffusing instruction among the poor, although he should oppose the further progress of this measure. . . . The provisions of the Bill left little or no control to the minister in his parish. This would go to subvert the first principles of education in this country, which had hitherto been, and he trusted would continue to be, under the control and auspices of the Establishment. . . .

From William Cobbett, *Parliamentary Debates*, IX.

Rural education

Hannah More, writing to the bishop of Bath and Wells, 1801, finds it necessary to assert her orthodoxy in explaining her Christian mission.

. . When I settled in this country thirteen years ago, I found the poor in many of the villages in a deplorable state of ignorance and vice. . . . My plan of instruction is extremely simple and limited. They learn, on week-days, such coarse works as may fit them for servants. I allow of no writing for the poor. My object is not to make fanatics but to train up the lower classes in habits of industry and piety. . . .

I need not inform your lordship why the illiterate, when they become religious, are more liable to enthusiasm than the better-informed. They have also a coarse way of expressing their religious sentiments, which often appears to be enthusiasm, when it is only vulgarity or quaintness. But I am persuaded that your lordship will allow that this does not furnish a reason why the poor should be left destitute of religious instruction. That the knowledge of the Bible should lay men more open to the delusions of fanaticism on the one hand, or of Jacobinism on the other, appears so unlikely, that I should have thought the probability lay all on the other side.

I do not vindicate enthusiasm, I dread it. But can the possibility that a few should become enthusiasts be justly pleaded as an argument for giving them all up to actual vice and barbarism?

From *Letters of Hannah More*. Selected by R. Brimley Johnson 1925. B.M. Shelfmark: 10906.666.17.

V. PRISONS

document 35

Model prison regulations, 1789

The intractable problem of prison reform produced rational and human discussion: John Howard's proposals incidentally portray existing conditions.

III. That until the laudable example of the county of Sussex . . in abolishing all fees, be generally adopted, a table of fees made by the Justices, and confirmed by the Judges, be also hung up in the prisons; and that no garnish, or any other fee but what is allowed as above, be permitted to be taken of any prisoner.

IV. That every prison be white-washed at least once in every year, and that this be done twice in prisons which are much crowded.

VI. That every prison be supplied with a warm and cold bath or commodious bathing tubs, and that the prisoners be indulged in the use of such baths, with a proper allowance of soap, and the use of towels.

VII. That attention be paid to the sewers, in order to render them as little offensive as possible.

VIII. That no animals of any kind which render a prison dirty be allowed to be kept in it, wither by the gaoler, or any prisoner. The only exception to this rule, should be one dog kept by the gaoler.

IX. That great care be taken, that as perfect a separation as possible be made of the following classes of prisoners, viz. That felons be kept entirely separate from debtors; men from women; old offenders from young beginners; and convicts from those who have not been tried.

X. That all prisoners, except debtors, be clothed on their admission with a prison uniform. . . .

XII. That no gaoler, or any person in trust to him, or employed by him, be permitted to sell any wine, beer, or other liquors, or permit or suffer any such to be sold in any prison; or on any pretext whatever, to suffer any tippling or gaming in the prison.
XIII. That a proper salary be given to the gaoler, in lieu of the profits which he formerly derived from the tap, from fees, and other perquisites.
XIV. That prisoners . . . be supplied with materials, and be allowed part of the profits (of such work . . .).
XV. That a clergyman be appointed. . . .
XVIII. That a surgeon or apothecary be appointed. . . .
XIX. That great attention be paid to what concerns the debtors, as it is found that that part of the management of our prisons has hitherto been most neglected.
XXII. That the prisons be frequently visited. . . .

From *An Account of the Present State of the Prisons . . . in London and Westminster. Taken from a late Publication of John Howard, Esq., F.R.S. by Permission of the Author:* a pamphlet.

VI. COMBINATION

document 36

Hosiers and framework knitters

Disturbances arising from unemployment were a plague to the magistrates, and the malign connection between outdoor relief, low wages, and union activity was generally assumed.

C. G. Mundy, J.P. to Viscount Sidmouth.
Burton, nr. Loughborough. 22 July 1817.

. . . The workmen supported by the parish officers who are of the opinion (and I fear with some truth) that there exists a combination among the hosiers to keep down the prices of the workmen so low that the parishes are obliged to make up the earnings of the workmen so as to enable them to support their families, & thus carry on their trade in some measure out of the poor rates . . . (13 August 1817) . . . a sort of warfare between the parish officers and the hosiers. . . . I fear these disputes may lead to dangerous combinations again on the part of the workmen.

HO 42/169.

document 37

Seamen

This handbill appeared during the powerless era when the workers, having lost the protection of paternalism, had yet to perfect the defensive system of unionism. The Combination Acts are here seen as a corrective sanction.

TWENTY GUINEAS REWARD

Whereas certain hand bills have been written and posted up against the walls in North Shields, calling a meeting of the seamen to consider of advancing the sailors' wages, NOTICE IS HEREBY GIVEN that a reward of TWENTY GUINEAS will be paid by the churchwardens and overseers of the parish of Tynemouth to any person or persons who will give such information to the magistrates as may lead to the conviction of the offender or offenders.

North Shields 12 September 1816

HO 42/153.

document 38

VII. CARE AND MAINTENANCE

This and the following document illustrate the careful attention received by the village's own poor, the most praiseworthy feature of the old Poor Law.

George Monk

George Monk, of Chalfont St Peter, Bucks, first appears as a small-holder, taking in a sick traveller, and subsequently has over 300 entries to himself.

124

			£	s.	d.
1739 June	The charg of George Monk to Bedlam			10	6
	& for ye Bonds & ye Clarke		1	1	0
	pd ye Steward for Beding		1	14	0
	pd to Mrs Bealy for ye Certificate			4	0
	pd ye porter & other tenders			5	0
	pd for a diner for ye Bondsmen and other expences with hors and men		2	15	6

George Monk stayed in Bedlam a few months, and moved back to the village in October. Thereafter he was in and out of the village cage, and his wife received a monthly pension of 4s. She died of smallpox in 1746, but pensions continued to his daughter, 'George Monk's Garl'. He continued to be sustained by the parish, as is shown by the following extracts:

		£	s.	d.
1748 Aug	Pd to Conn Hunt for 6 Ells of Doules for George Monk for 2 shurts		5	6
1750 Jan	Paid to Jane Garman for loocking after George Monk in ye keag (cage)		2	0
1750 Apr	paid for one truss of straw for G. Monk			6
1751 May	Given George Monk upon his walk			6
1752 Sep	paid for a wascote & shurt & making & Breches making & 1 new Sickle for G.M.		7	6
	Bought him a new kittle		1	6
Nov	Paid for a new fowlwether for Geo. Monk		14	2
1754 Feb	Paid for a tinn quart pott & 2 nives for him			8
Mar	paid for a lock and chaine for Geo. Monk		5	6
1755 Mar	Given George Monk		3	4½
	Paid the bearing of George Monk		16	0
1759 Sep	Paid for 2 handkerchiefs for monks garl			7

From an article by Geoffrey C. Edmonds in *Records of Buckinghamshire*, vol. 38, part 1, 1966 (**60**).

Jo Skinner

Jo Skinner of the parish of Wimbledon is another typical recipient of community. Some of the entries are bleak in tone, but attention is consistent, and probably more involved than a buff-coloured form might be.

29 June 1746	Jo Skinner 2 shirts.
26 Dec 1746	Jo Skinner a coat, a pr of breeches a 1 pr of shoes and stockings.
25 Oct 1747	Jo Skinner 2 shirts and a coarse sheet.
26 Dec 1747	Jo Skinner a shirt and a pr of shoes.
13 Mar 1748	Jo Skinner allowed relief at the discretion of the officers.
12 Apr 1748	Jo Skinner to be allowed no relief, for it is the opinion of the vestry that he is capable of doing something for a livelihood.
14 May 1748	Jo Skinner allowed no relief, for it is the opinion of the vestry that (he) is capable of getting (his) own living.
19 June 1748	Jo Skinner allowed 1s. 6d. p.w. pension, 4 lbs. of meat every week, a kettle to boil his meat in, a pr of drawers and 1 pr of stockings.
25 Sept 1748	Pension list settled for winter. Jo Skinner 1s. 6d.
29 Jan 1749	Jo Skinner allowed 2 shirts.
24 Sept 1749	Jo Skinner 1 shirt, but it is to be stopped out of his pension at 6d. p.w. for 5 weeks.
26 Dec 1749	Jo Skinner allowed 1 shirt and 1 pr of shoes.
14 May 1750	Pension settled for the summer half-year. Jo Skinner 1s.
4 Nov 1750	Jo Skinner allowed 1 foulweather coat, 2 shirts, 1 pr of shoes and stockings, and 2d. a week to be stopped out of his pension by the overseers for washing his linen to keep him clean.
9 Apr 1751	Phillis Bowen allowed 5s. for nursing and laying out Jo Skinner.
5 May 1751	Ro. Colyer may have Jo Skinner's foulweather coat and shoes and Wi. Westbrook his 2 old shirts and breeches.

The cost of Jo Skinner to the Vestry in his last year of life. From the Overseers' Accounts, 1750–51:

	£	s.	d.
pd John Skinner . . . 47 weeks at 1s. per week	2	7	0
pd for a Foulweather Coat for John Skinner	0	16	0
pd for a Pair of Stockings for Ditto	0	1	0
pd for 2 Shirts and Making for Ditto	0	6	0
pd James Jennings for a Pair of Breeches for John Skinner	0	5	0
pd for Coals, Candles, Cinnamon and Sugar for John Skinner while Ill	0	1	6
pd William Coatsworth for Wine and Beer for John Skinner had in his Illness	0	2	3¼
pd the Widow Bowen for Nurssing him	0	5	0
pd the parsons and Clarks fees & four Men for Carrying him to Church and for Bread, cheese and beer had att his Buriall	0	11	6
	4	13	3¼

From *Wimbledon Vestry Minutes, SRO P5/5/8.*

VIII. A POOR MAN'S PLEA

document 40

Cost of burial

Such a record is rare, since it was left by a poor man. This application for relief from Gnosall, Staffs., is dated 12 December 1812.

Jeantlemen at this time I ham In grate distress my youngest son is dad and I have another doughter vury bad and I my sealfe am hill Sir the cofin will be 12s. and the ground with the fees will be 5s. 6d. and the shroud 3s. 6d. Sir threaugh stoping my trifle of pay I have 14s. in det for seame and if not paid by christmas I must be trioubled Jeantlemen I hope you will not stop my trifle of pay at this time your humble servant

Thos. Bannister

(endorsed)

Mr. Haynes. It appears by this letter that one of Bannister's Child[n] are dead, I think it will be necessary to allow him something towards burying it about one pound and take care of this note

Yrs

etc

Jos. Taylor

14th. Dec. 1822

The Child's name is Enoch—(in another hand) Gave him a Pound Note.

From S. A. Cutlack (59).

Bibliography

ORIGINAL SOURCES

Documentation is so copious as to give the student an exceptional freedom from secondary sources: it is not obligatory to read 'historians repeating each other'. Much work remains to be done by local historians, indeed, since the 15,000 parishes which formerly supported the Poor Laws left records, many of which await discovery. The use of such material is best explained in W. E. Tate, *The Parish Chest* (**41**), and W. G. Hoskins, *Local History in England and Wales* (**23**). Among published records, the following have been most helpful:

English Historical Documents, vols. viii, x, xi, xii.

Aspinall, A., *The Early English Trade Unions*. Oxford Univ. Press. 1949.

Cole, G. D. H. and Filson, A. W., *British Working Class Movements. Select Documents*.

Cowe, F. M., ed. *Wimbledon Vestry Minutes, 1736, 1763–1788*, Surrey Record Society, vol. 25.

Peet, Henry, ed. *Liverpool Vestry Books, 1681–1834*. Liverpool University Press, 1912.

The *Victoria County Histories* provide a useful starting point, but Quarter Sessions Papers are a richer, if less accessible, quarry. The Public Record Office holds the Chatham Papers and the Home Office Papers, and the British Museum contains all of the tracts mentioned, and much else. Newspapers and periodicals give perhaps the most alluring introduction to the workings of the Poor Laws, and the subject will be found to occupy the news columns of the provincial press, besides providing advertising copy. The *Gentleman's Magazine* (from 1731) and *The Annual Register* (from 1758) comment on the national scene, and *The Weekly Political Register* voices Cobbett's highly personalised views on the poor. Aris's *Birmingham Gazette* has been an additional aid to the present work.

Bibliography

GENERAL

The problem of pauperism is intrinsic to eighteenth century society, and is so well covered that the list below refers only to those works used in the text. The chronologically relevant volumes of the Oxford Histories, for example, do not appear, although they deal with the subject to a more or less extent. Some of the books cited are peripheral, nonetheless: the one indispensable work is that of the Webbs, whose *Old Poor Law* (**49**) is but one volume of their awesome contribution to the history of English local government. Miss Marshall's balanced judgment (**32**) is to be set against the impassioned, immaculately stylish, writings of the Hammonds (**17, 18, 19**). The most particular account of several aspects of poverty is to be found in Dr George's compelling study of the people of eighteenth-century London (**14**). Curiously, the problem excites comparatively little controversy, and those moved by contention would best look at the articles of Mark Blaug (**55, 56**).

Books

1   Ashton, T. S. *An Economic History of England: The Eighteenth Century*, Oxford University Press 1948.
2   Aspinall, A. *The Early English Trade Unions*, Oxford University Press 1949.
3   Barley, M. W. *The English Farmhouse and Cottage*, Routledge & Kegan Paul 1961.
4   Beloff, Max. *Public Order and Popular Disturbances, 1660–1714*, Frank Cass 1963.
5   Briggs, Asa. *The Age of Improvement, 1780–1867*, Longmans 1959.
6   Buer, M. C. *Health, Wealth and Population*, new edn. Routledge 1968.
7   Chambers, J. D. and Mingay, G. E. *The Agricultural Revolution, 1750–1880*, Batsford 1966.
8   Cipolla, C. *A History of World Population*, Penguin 1962.
9   Clapham, J. H. *An Economic History of Modern Britain: The Early Railway Age*, Cambridge University Press 1927.
10 Cole, G. D. H. and Postgate, R. *The Common People*, Methuen 1946.
11 Deane, Phyllis. *The First Industrial Revolution*, Cambridge University Press 1965.

12 Ede, J. F. *History of Wednesbury*, The Kynoch Press 1962.

13 George, Dorothy. *England in Transition*, Penguin 1953.

14 George, Dorothy. *London Life in the Eighteenth Century*, Kegan Paul 1925.

15 Gilboy, E. W. *Wages in Eighteenth-Century England*, Harvard University Press 1934.

16 Halévy, E., *England in 1815*, Vol. I of *A History of the English People in the Nineteenth Century*, Ernest Benn 1949.

17 Hammond, J. L. and Hammond, B. *The Village Labourer* (1911), Longmans 1966.

18 Hammond, J. L. and Hammond, B. *The Town Labourer* (1917), Longmans 1966.

19 Hammond, J. L. and Hammond, B. *The Skilled Labourer* (1919), Longmans 1948.

20 Hanson, L. W. *Government and the Press, 1695–1763*, Oxford University Press 1936 (reprint 1967).

21 Hill, C. P. *The Century of Revolution*, Nelson 1961.

22 Hill, C. P. *Reformation to Industrial Revolution*, Weidenfeld & Nicolson 1967.

23 Hoskins, W. G. *Local History in England*, Longmans 1959.

24 Hoskins, W. G. *The Midland Peasant*, Macmillan 1957

25 Howard, D. L. *John Howard, Prison Reformer*, Christopher Johnson 1958.

26 Jones, M. G. *The Charity School Movement: A study of eighteenth-century puritanism in action*, Cambridge University Press 1938.

27 Jordan, W. K. *Philanthropy in England, 1480–1660*, Allen & Unwin 1959.

28 Leonard, E. M. *Early History of the Poor Law*, Frank Cass 1965.

29 Lipson, E. *The Economic History of England*, vol. 3: *The Age of Mercantilism*, A. and C. Black 1947.

30 Mantoux, Paul. *The Industrial Revolution in the Eighteenth Century*, Cape 1947.

31 Marshall, D. *The English Poor in the Eighteenth Century*, Routledge 1926.

32 Marshall, D. *English People in the Eighteenth Century*, Longmans 1956.

33 Mathias, Peter. *The Brewing Industry in England, 1700–1830*, Cambridge University Press 1959.

34 Midwinter, E. C. *Victorian Social Reform*, Longmans (*Seminar Studies in History*) 1968.

131

35 Namier, L. B. *England in the Age of the American Revolution*, Macmillan 1930.

36 Nicholls, Sir George. *A History of the English Poor Law*, London 1854.

37 Owen, David. *English Philanthropy, 1660–1960*, Oxford University Press 1965.

38 Rudé, G. *The Crowd in History*, John Wiley 1964.

39 Sykes, N. *Church and State in England in the Eighteenth Century*, Cambridge University Press 1934.

40 Tate, W. E. *The Parish Chest*, Cambridge University Press 1946.

41 Tate. W. E. *The English Village Community*, Gollancz 1967.

42 Tawney, R. H. *Religion and the Rise of Capitalism*, Penguin 1938.

43 Thompson, E. P. *The Making of the English Working Class*, Gollancz 1963.

44 Trevelyan, G. M. *Illustrated English Social History*, Longmans 1950.

45 Trotter, E. *Seventeenth-Century Life in the Country Parish*, Cambridge University Press 1919.

46 Wearmouth, R. F. *Methodism and the Common People of the Eighteenth Century*, Epworth Press 1945.

47 Webb, S. and Webb, B. *The Parish and the County*, Vol. I of *English Local Government*, Frank Cass 1963.

48 Webb, S. and Webb, B. *English Prisons under Local Government*, Vol. 6 of *English Local Government*, Frank Cass 1963.

49 Webb, S. and Webb, B. *English Poor Law History*, Vol. 7 of *English Local Government*, Frank Cass 1963.

50 Webb, S. and Webb, B. *The Rise of Trade Unionism*, Chiswick Press 1911.

51 Weber, Max *The Protestant Ethic and the Spirit of Capitalism*, Unwin (University Books) 1930.

52 Wilson, C. *England's Apprenticeship*, Longmans 1965.

A recent publication too late to include in the text discusses the Swing Riots. It is Hobsbawn, E. J. and Rudé, G. *Captain Swing*, Lawrence and Wishart, 1969.

Articles

53 Ashby, A. W. 'A hundred years of Poor Law in a Warwickshire village', *Oxford Studies in Social and Legal History*, vol. iii, 66.

54 Beier, A. L. 'Poor relief in Warwickshire, 1630–1660', *Past and Present*, 35, 1966.

55 Blaug, M. 'Myth of the Old Poor Law and making of the New', *Journal of Economic History*, vol. 13 June 1963.

56 Blaug, M. 'Poor Law Report re-examined', *Journal of Economic History*, vol. 14 June 1964.

57 Butcher, E. E. 'Bristol Corporation of the Poor—Records, 1696–1834', *Bristol Record Soc. Pubs.*, 1932.

58 Chambers, J. D. 'The Vale of Trent, 1670–1800', *Economic History Review*, Supplemennt No. 3 Cambridge University Press.

59 Cutlack, S. A. 'The Gnosall Records, 1679–1837', Staffordshire Record Society, 1936.

60 Edmonds, G. C. 'Accounts of C18 overseers of the poor of Chalfont St. Peter', *Records of Buckinghamshire* vol. 18, part 1, 1966.

61 Emmison, F. G. 'The relief of the poor in Eaton Socon, 1706–1832', *Bedfordshire Historical Record Society*, vol. 15, 1933.

62 Glass, D. V. 'Gregory King's estimate of the population of England and Wales, 1695', *Population Studies*, 1949–50.

63 Habakkuk, H. J. 'English population in the eighteenth century', *Economic History Review*, 2nd series, vol. 6, no. 2, 1953.

64 Hampson, E. M. 'Treatment of poverty in Cambridgeshire, 1597–1834', 1934.

65 Hill, C. 'Puritans and the poor', *Past and Present*, no. 2, 195?.

66 Hobsbawn, E. J. 'The machine breakers', *Past and Present*, no. 1, 1952.

67 Marshall, D. 'Old Poor Law, 1662–1795', in *Essays in Economic History*, vol. I, Edward Arnold 1954.

68 Marshall, T. H. 'The population problem during the industrial revolution. (A Note on the Present State of the Controversy)', *Essays in Economic History*, vol. I, Edward Arnold 1961.

69 Neate, A. R. 'The St Marylebone Workhouse and Institution, 1730–1965', *St Marylebone Society Publication*, no. 9, 1967.

70 Oldham, C. R. 'Oxfordshire Poor Law papers', *Economic History Review*, vols. 4, 5, 1934.

71 Plumb, J. H. 'Sir Robert Walpole's Wines', in *Men and places*, Cresset 1963.

72 Rudé, G. 'English rural and urban disturbance on the eve of the first Reform Bill, 1830–1831', *Past and Present*, no. 37, 1967.

73 Sheppard, F. H. W., *History Today*, London before the L.C.C. March 1953.

74 Silberling, N. J. 'British prices and business cycles, 1779–1850', *Review of Economic Statistics*, 1923.

Bibliography

75 Stone, L. and Everitt, Alan 'Social mobility', *Past and Present* no. 35, 1966.

76 Taylor, A. J. Progress and poverty in Britain, 1780–1850 *History*, vol. 45, 1960.

77 Thomas, K. 'Work and leisure in pre-industrial Society' (Past and Present Conference Paper), 29, 1964.

78 Viner, 'Man's economic status', in *Man versus Society in eighteenth century Britain*, Cambridge University Press, 1968.

79 White, R. J. 'The Lower Classes of Regency England', *History Today*, Sept. 1963.

80 Wilson, C. 'The other face of mercantilism', *Transactions of the Royal Historical Society*, 5th series, vol. 9, 1959.

CONTEMPORARY WRITINGS

The proliferation of such material compensates for the shortage of statistics. Any list must necessarily be selective, and the under mentioned indicate only a basis for study.

81 Alcock, Thomas. *Observations on Defects of the Poor Laws*, 1752.

82 Bamford, Samuel. *Passages in the Life of a Radical*, Heywood 1841.

83 Burn, R. *History of the Poor Laws; with observations*, 1764

84 Burn, R. *The J.P. and the Parish Officer*, 1755.

85 Cary, John. *An Essay on the State of England in relation to its Trade its Poor and its Taxes*, 1695.

86 Child, Sir Josiah. *New Discourse of Trade*, 1670.

87 Cobbett, W. *Rural Rides*, 1830 (Dent, Everyman 1953.)

88 Davenant. *Essays upon Ways and Means*, 1695.

89 Davies, Rev. D. *The Case of Labourers in Husbandry, stated and considered*, 1795.

90 Defoe, Daniel. *Giving Alms No Charity, and employing the Poor a grievance to the Nation*, 1704.

91 Dunning, Richard. *Bread for the poor or, a method shewing how the poor may be maintained*, 1698.

92 Eden, Sir F. M. *The State of the Poor*, 1797. (Abridged ed. with intro. by A. G. C. Rogers, 1928).

93 Fielding, H. *A Proposal for Making an Effectual Provision for the Poor*, 1753.

134

94 Firmin, Thomas. *Some Proposals for the Employment of the Poor and for the Prevention of Idleness & the Consequences thereof, Beggary,* 1678.

95 Gilbert, Thos. *A Scheme for the Better Relief and Employment of the poor,* 1764 (1st January).

96 Haines, Richard. *The Prevention of Poverty, or a Discourse of the Causes of the Decay of Trade,* 1674.

97 Hale, Sir Matthew. *A Discourse Touching Provision for the Poor,* 1663.

98 Hanway, Jonas. *An Earnest Appeal for Mercy to the Children of the Poor,* 1766.

99 Howard, D. *The State of the Prisons in England and Wales,* 1780.

100 Hutton, William. *Life,* 1816.

101 King, Gregory. *Natural and Political Observations and Conclusions upon the State and Condition of England,* 1696.

102 Locke, John. *A Report of the Board of Trade to the Lords Justices respecting the Relief and Employment of the Poor,* 1697.

103 Malthus, Rev. Thomas. *Essay on the Principle of Population as it affects the future Improvement of Society,* 1798.

104 Petty, Sir William. *Essays on Political Arithmetick,* 1672.

105 Ricardo. *Principles of Political Economy and Taxation,* 1817.

106 Ruggles, Thos. *The History of the Poor, their rights, duties, and the laws respecting them,* 1793–1794.

107 Smith, Adam. *The Wealth of Nations,* 1776.

108 Townsend, Joseph. *A dissertation on the poor laws,* 1786.

109 Wesley, J. *Journal,* ed. N. Curnock, Epworth Press 1909.

110 Woodforde. *Diary of a Country Parson 1758–1802,* Oxford University Press (World's Classics) 1949.

111 Young, Arthur. *Annals of Agriculture,* 1784–1809.

112 Young, Arthur. *Northern Tour,* 1770.

LITERATURE

While works of fiction require careful treatment as historical evidence, references to the problems discussed in this book are too frequent to be wholly neglected. Contemporary writers evoke an atmosphere which stimulates the imagination, besides themselves contributing to current attitudes. It is not possible here to reproduce a full bibliography, and it is right that the student should follow his own senses in this subjective field.

The eighteenth century produced, out of its rationalism, a regard for truth and reality which previous centuries had expressed in other terms, allegorical or representative. The novel, particularly, gave new form to expression, and its initiators stretched its possibilities to incorporate new subjects.

By far the most significant writer in this respect was Henry Fielding, whose *The History of Tom Jones, a Foundling*, 1749, *Joseph Andrews*, 1742, and *Amelia*, 1751, had a didactic purpose to promote virtue, in considering poverty. He was a moralist who regarded luxury as the lurking enemy of the poor, expressed by Pope, whose Satan 'tempts by making rich, not making poor'. The discipline of his outlook and particularly his sympathy with debtors reveal the still present middle-class conflict between moral values and social materialism. Fielding did not ease his own dilemma by asserting the doctrine of the natural goodness of man: Blifil is a creation of pre-disposed wickedness, while Jones, his half-brother and similarly educated by the ridiculous Thwackum, was characterised by innate goodness: such antithesis was at the root of Fielding's morality. His experience as a J.P. at the Middlesex Sessions gave Fielding's comments informed authority and his description of the conspiracy of Lady Booby and Lawyer Scout, to deny Andrews a settlement, employs the biting weapon of truth.

Fielding's influence on the spirit of humanitarianism was inestimable, and his awareness of social conditions was such that it required no further advocacy than mere assertion, presaging the silent testaments of nineteenth-century Royal Commissions. To a group of interested M.P.s, who requested a tour through the London slums, Fielding said:

If we were to make a progress through the outskirts of this town, and look into the habitations of the poor, we should there behold such pictures of human misery as must move the compassion of every heart that deserves the name of human ... whole families in want of every necessary of life, oppressed with hunger, cold, nakedness, and filth, and with diseases ... who could look on a scene such as this, and be affected only in his nostrils? That such wretchedness as this is so little lamented, arises therefore from its being so little known, but if this be the case with the sufferings of the poor, it is not so with their misdeeds. They starve, and freeze, and rot among themselves; but they beg and steal, and rob among their betters.

136

The common sense of Doctor Johnson, 'Slow rises Worth, by Poverty deprest' (*London*, 1738), with its acceptance of material standards mollified by a kindly disposition, was a unique contribution to his, and indeed to any other, age. His *bon mots* are too numerous even to sample, but his insistence (found in Boswell's *The Life of Samuel Johnson*, 1791) on the supremacy of England in treating the poor is interesting, and a little comical in view of his prejudices against foreigners: 'He said, the poor in England were better provided for, than in any other country of the same extent. . . . Gentlemen of education, he observed, were pretty much the same in all countries; the condition of the lower orders, the poor especially, was the true mark of national discrimination'. The sentiment recalls de Tocqueville's distorted impression that tax evasion was the privilege of the nobility in France, the poor in England.

Goldsmith's *Vicar of Wakefield* (1766) is more universal, and less suspect a work than his *Deserted Village* (1770). The travails of the righteous family are treated with a sympathy utterly consistent with the changing character of the age, and his preference for the lower orders anticipates Dickens. The solid qualities of simple folk make a moving and timeless impression: his wise man's prayer was 'Give me not poverty, lest I steal.' *The Deserted Village* is nevertheless worth scrutiny, and supports Fielding's diagnosis of the plague of poverty:

> Ill fares the land, to hast'ning ills a prey,
> Where wealth accumulates, and men decay;
> . . .
> A time there was, ere England's griefs began,
> When every rood of ground maintain'd its man;
> For him light labour spread her wholesome store,
> Just gave what life requir'd, but gave no more;
> His best companions, innocence and health;
> And his best riches, ignorance of wealth.

Goldsmith experienced financial hardship himself, and he knew the insecurity of a parson's family, but perhaps the knowledge of poverty bit more deeply into the personality of George Crabbe.

Crabbe's pessimism did not allow him the indulgent backward glance of Goldsmith, the poesy of nostalgia. Crabbe's penchant was for a realism whose starkness would fit the present century, and his Orwellian fancy for description omitted no mournful scene, no sombre detail. His pen was specially fine, and wrote of minutiae with

137

care. But he always used black ink, and so his picture was harsh and incomplete. As a contrast to roseate cottages and ruddy-cheeked peasants, his delineations are sharpening and invaluable to the social historian. *The Village* (1783), *The Parish Register* (1807), and *The Borough* (1810), read in conjunction with Gilbert White's *The Natural History of Selborne* (1798) and John Langhorne's *The Country Justice* (1774), conjure an acceptable impression of rural life. Crabbe's portrayal of the village poor house has become almost a standard text and exceeds Dickens in realism, if not in sentimental appeal:

> Theirs is yon house that holds the parish-poor,
> Whose walls of mud scarce bear the broken door;
> There, where the putrid vapours, flagging, play,
> And the dull wheel hums doleful through the day;
> There children dwell who know no parents' care;
> Parents, who know no children's love, dwell there! . . .
> The lame, the blind, and, far the happiest they!
> The moping idiot and the madman gay.
> Here too the sick their final doom receive,
> Here brought, amid the scenes of grief, to grieve . . .
> Here, sorrowing, they each kindred sorrow scan,
> And the cold charities of man to man.

A delightful work by Mary Russell Mitford, *Our Village, sketches of rural character and scenery, 1819–1832*, contains a prose picture of a village workhouse:

> That large heavy building on one side of the common, whose solid wings, jutting out far beyond the main body, occupy three sides of a square and give a cold, shadowy look to the Court. On one side is a gloomy garden with an old man digging in it, laid out in straight dark beds of vegetables, potatoes, cabbages, onions, beans all earthy and mouldy as a newly-dug grave. Not a flower or flowering shrub! Not a rose-tree or currant-bush! . . . That is the parish workhouse. All about it is solid, substantial, useful; but so dreary! so cold! so dark! There are children in the court, and yet all is silent . . . yet, perhaps, if not certainly, they contain less of that extreme desolation than the morbid fancy is apt to paint. There will be found order, cleanliness, food, clothing, warmth; refuge for the homeless, medicine and attendance for the sick; rest and sufficiency for old age, and sympathy, the true and active

sympathy which the poor show to the poor, for the unhappy. There may be worse places than the parish workhouse—and yet I hurry past it.

Miss Mitford's writing has the authenticity of the diarist, and of this genre Parson Woodforde is the supreme eighteenth-century instance. As a country cleric, he lived close to the poor, and doled out money in regular dribs and drabs: 'To a very poor Weaver with a large Family and a Wife and can get no Work whatever gave last Night 0.1.0.' Each St Thomas's Day, year after year, he gave to the poor their Christmas gifts—usually 6*d*. His charity was touched equally by compassion and caution:

July 15, Thursday. To a poor Woman from Dereham by name Hall with a small Child with her was taken very ill with a violent Pain within her by my great Gates and was laid down in the road, I went out and gave her a good Glass of Gin and gave her sixpence to go to the Inn. . . . She is a Widow and belongs to the House of Industry near Dereham. I hope she is no Impostor.

The poor's utter dependence on some perishable property was shown in the entry of 15 December 1791, 'To one John Sparkes of Eastn past 72 years a Labourer, having lost his only Hobby which used to carry him to his work at Honingham he being a Brick-Maker, gave 2.6'. The *Diary* throughout its pages, gives fascinating glimpses of the lives of ordinary people, showing them, among other things, to enjoy some mobility, however precarious:

27 *October, 1792*. To a Man . . . who escaped this morning out of Bargewell's Poor House being hardly kept alive there . . . the House being farmed out at 1ˢ/6ᵈ per Week for each poor Person . . . gave 0.1.0. He was going for London.
27 *November, 1793*. To a poor Kentish Man who goes about the country and plays Tunes on the Church-Bells, gave 0.1.0.
7 *July, 1794* To a poor Sailor having lost his left hand, gave 1.0.·

His last St Thomas's Day distribution, in 1800, found the poor behaving 'extremely well indeed', 'very patient and submissive', although 'times were extremely hard for them'. This simple man's world, hierarchical yet communally involved, is unforgettably charted, and excites anger and admiration in varying proportions.

Other observers of those poor people unable to leave their own records were Defoe and Cobbett, and a similarly descriptive theme marks several other of the early novelists, notably Smollett.

The Romantics, too, with their radical political views—which surely owed something to the extended exercise of imagination—and a new reverence for common humanity, colour the period in its later stages. William Blake, isolated and intuitive, identified with the oppressed, and with the young. *The Songs of Experience* shows an appreciation of the charity school parade:

'Twas on a Holy Thursday, their innocent faces clear,
The children walking two and two, in red and blue and green.

He was naturally drawn to the child sweep's plight:

When my mother died I was very young,
And my father sold me while yet my tongue
Could scarcely cry ' 'weep! 'weep! 'weep! 'weep!'
So your chimneys I sweep, and in soot I sleep.

Wordsworth, leader of the movement, saw the poor as a vehicle for inducing virtuous charity: having given money to Alice Fell, a freezing orphan girl, he anticipates the effect of his benevolence: 'Proud creature was she the next day.' Similarly, he dramatised the condition of beggary in *The Sailor's Mother*, 'majestic in her person, tall and straight', and in *Beggars*, 'towered, fit person for a Queen'. Those who receive were equally a part of Wordsworth's natural order as those who gave:

these inevitable charities,
Wherewith to satisfy the human soul.
No—man is dear to man, the poorest poor.
. . .
Themselves, the fathers and the dealers out
Of some small blessings . . .

This complacent view is emphasised by his old man, 'stately in the main', who maintains himself in age and infirmity by gathering leeches in ponds (*Resolution and Independence*), and the Old Cumberland Beggar is praised for keeping clear of the 'House, misnamed of Industry' which threatened to make him a captive. Wordsworth saw no improvement in such institutions, which might deprive society of opportunities for charity, and his whole concept of poverty moulds mpathy in the setting of acceptance. Like the Cumberland beggar, maybe, Wordsworth had 'his eyes for ever on the ground'.

The historian who ignores such writings will be the poorer, for e will find no compensating comfort in statistics—there are no ighteenth-century Blue Books, no literate poor, to furnish evidence. he literature of the period introduces a new strain of realism, angible as Colling's shorthorn, and makes strong claims to consideration as serious material for study. And if it fails to quantify any istorical problem, it will at least nourish historical empathy.